Rethinking Jesus:
When the Walk Fails the Talk

The way to see by faith is to shut the eye of reason.
—Benjamin Franklin

Rethinking Jesus:
When the Walk Fails the Talk

Dennis R. Blue

Inara Publishing
An Imprint of GCRR Press
1312 17th Street Suite 549
Denver, CO 80202

INFO@GCRR.ORG • INARAPUBLISHING.COM

Inara Publishing
An imprint of GCRR Press
1312 17th Street Suite 549
Denver, CO 80202
www.inarapublishing.com

Copyright © 2021 by Dennis R. Blue

All rights reserved. No part of this publication may be reproduced, stored in a retrieval system, or transmitted in any form or by any means, electronic, mechanical, photocopying, recording, or otherwise, without the prior permission of GCRR Press. For permissions, contact: info@gcrr.org.

Unless otherwise noted, Scripture quotations are from "The Holy Bible," New King James Version, copyright © 1982 Thomas Nelson, Inc., a division of Harper Collins Christian Publishing, Inc. Used by permission. All rights reserved worldwide.

Typesetter/Copyeditor/Proofreader: Christian Farren
Cover Design: Abdullah Al Mahmud
        fiverr.com/mahmuddidar

Library of Congress Cataloging-in-Publication Data

Rethinking Jesus: when the walk fails the talk / Dennis R. Blue
p.   cm.
Includes bibliographic references (p.).
ISBN (Print): 978-1-7378469-3-2
ISBN (eBook): 978-1-7378469-4-9
1. Christianity—Controversial literature.   2. Jesus Christ.   3. Bible—Criticism, interpretation, etc.   I. Title.

BS2350-2393   .B584   2021

This book is dedicated to the vast number of sincere individuals who have given Christianity a place in their lives, only to become disillusioned and discouraged by its moribund shortcomings.

Contents

Preface   xi

1 Jesus of Nazareth   1

    Daniel's Prophecy   2
    Mary's Controversial Conception   2
    Mary and Elizabeth: Manufacturing an Explanation   3
    Virgin Birth and Medical Considerations   5
    Yeshua ben Pantera   6
    Hebrew Monotheism and the Holy Spirit   7
    Missing the Messianic Mark   8
    Genetics and Davidic Lineage   9
    The Blood Curse of Jeconiah   10
    Commentary   11

2 The Birth of Jesus   13

    Bethlehem   13
    The Nativity Story   14
    The Magi   16
    What's in a Name?   19
    Growing Up   21
    Commentary   22

3 Gathering Followers   24

    Undivided Devotion   26
    More on the Family   28
    "Follow Me"   28

      Hometown Repudiation   29
      The Modern Follower of Jesus   30
      Commentary   32

4   The Sanity of the Savior   34

      Early Observations   35
      Schizophrenia   36
      The Mind of Jesus—What Others Thought   38
      Narcissism   38
      Demon Possession   40
      Commentary   42

5   The Ministry of Jesus   44

      Miracles   45
      The Miracle at Cana   48
      Modern Magic   50
      The Jesus Seminars   51
      Preaching and Teaching   52
      Commentary   53

6   Creating the Savior Paradigm   56

      The Impossible Role: Savior and Messiah   57
      Supersessionism   59
      False Prophet and False Messiah   61
      Who Am I?   62
      The Rejected Argument and the Rejected Messiah   63
      The Mount of Olives   64
      Empty Promises   66
      Commentary   67

7   The Crucifixion   69

      The Betrayal?   71
      The Money Changers   73

    The Garden   74
    The Cross   76
    Zombies for Jesus   79
    Historical Fact or Fiction?   80
    Three Days and Three Nights?   80
    Commentary   82

8   Is He Risen?   84

    Matthew   85
    Mark   85
    Luke   86
    John   87
    Will the Real Resurrection Account
       Please Stand Up?   88
    Commentary   89

9   Post-Resurrection Appearances and the Ascension   91

    Matthew   92
    Mark   92
    Luke   93
    John   94
    Paul   95
    The Gospel According to Matthew   97
    The Gospel According to Mark   97
    The Gospel According to Luke   98
    The Gospel According to John   98
    The Acts of the Apostles-Paul   99
    Commentary   99

10   The Talpiot Tomb   101

    Commentary   105

11	Was Jesus Married?	106
12	Contrasting the Hebrew Bible and the Christian Old Testament	109

    Scriptural Revision   110
    Immanuel and Isaiah 7:14   110
    The Red Sea Crossing   111
    David and Goliath   112
    Paul's Deception   113

13	The Physical Jesus	115
14	The Son of Aten and the Many Sons of Gods	118
15	Belief	120

    Belief, Emotions, and Mental Health   120
    Religious Trauma Syndrome   123
    Cognitive Dissonance   123
    Philosophy and Beliefs   124
    Scientific Investigation   125
    Patternicity and Conditioning   127
    Divided We Fall   128
    Commentary   130

Closing Thoughts	132
Bibliography	135

But when his own people heard about this, they went out to lay hold of Him, for they said 'He is out of His mind.'

Mark 3:21

Preface

For those of you whose lives are filled with spiritual doubts, or who are conflicted and torn about what to believe…For the many of you who are unable to reconcile the expectations that come from trusting Jesus with your spiritual station in life…For those who find yourselves emotionally exhausted by the constant testing of your faith—who must rationalize nonsensical circumstances with excuses, unlikely explanations, and denials…For the disheartened whose prayers do not get answered—whose doubts seem legitimate, but who are afraid to act on them…Most importantly, for those who have looked back on their Christian life and felt little but disappointment and failure…*Rethinking Jesus* was written for you.

This book is designed to provide encouragement and confidence, toward the end that it frees readers from doubt and fear—the hope being that you can modify or even walk away from your faith if you choose to. It does this by providing a cognitive understanding of Jesus that is unbiased and closer to truth. It re-examines the story of the self-appointed Messiah: an impostor who used hope as a tease.

You may be surprised to find that the unadulterated story of Jesus varies significantly from the one most Christians are familiar with. For centuries, Christian teachers and expositors have routinely cherry-picked the New Testament in their attempt to articulate a coherent tale of "the Lord" to an unsuspecting world. Their misguided efforts have beguiled many hope-filled believers whose lives do not reflect what they are being told. Taking a critical look at what they omit and fail to teach brings a new perspective to the table.

Rethinking Jesus is meant to restore readers' view of reality and return them to a rational frame of reference. It will remove the blinders from those whose vision of truth has been narrowed and distorted. This book offers a different look at the counterfeit Christ and the religion he created. It is unabashed in doing so. May it be eye-opening for some and life-changing for others.

—DB

Jesus of Nazareth

No one in history has had a greater impact on humankind than Jesus of Nazareth. His influence is pervasive even now, some two thousand years after he walked the earth. At the same time, there is likely no one who has generated more controversy than Jesus. Wars have been fought and millions have died over the question of who he was and what authority he should be granted in the lives of individuals, their cultures, and their civilizations. Even today, Christianity continues to impact and influence society at a multitude of levels.

Who was Jesus? *It has been said that Jesus was either who he claimed to be, or he was the greatest impostor in human history.* Author and Christian apologist C.S. Lewis wrote: "The man we are talking about either was (and is) just what he said, or something worse."[1]

We all know the basics of who Jesus said he was. He was unabashed in claiming to be the Hebrew Messiah, the Savior, and the only begotten Son of God.

However, when considering the intent of this book, we are compelled to view the life of Jesus from a different and more comprehensive perspective—one that is open-minded and willing to be harshly critical when necessary. We will boldly test biblical assertions and question authenticity where veracity seems lacking. Our sources will extend beyond the New Testament to external ports of information that are both plausible and reliable. Let us apply a critical eye to the complete and unadulterated story of Jesus. Who was this Jewish carpenter, really?

To understand how the worldview of Jesus developed into what it is now, necessity requires that we first examine the backdrop

---

[1] Lewis, *Mere Christianity*, 55–56.

of the time in which he lived. A Hebrew prophecy set the stage for the life of Jesus, who called himself the Christ.

Daniel's Prophecy

The prophecy found in Daniel 9 is arguably the most important in the Hebrew Bible. It begins with a prophecy in the book of Jeremiah that speaks to the captivity of the Jews in Babylonia. Daniel was given the new prophecy by an angel in 536 BCE. *Daniel prophesied that from the time of a decree authorizing the rebuilding of Jerusalem (the Babylonians had destroyed it), there would be "seventy weeks of seven" before the Messiah would appear.* It was understood that those 490 days represented 490 years.[2]

There were four decrees that surfaced regarding this prophecy. Only one of them was the true decree. The first was issued by Cyrus, the king of Persia, in 538 BCE. The second was given by Darius I of Persia in 519 BCE. The third and fourth decrees were issued by Artaxerxes, king of Persia, in 444 BCE and 457 BCE. It is the majority opinion of Bible scholars that the decree issued in 444 BCE approximates the date when Jesus began his ministry at age 30. Four hundred and ninety years following the third decree of Artaxerxes yields a date of 46 CE. Therefore, Daniel's prophecy for the appearance of the Messiah turned out to be roughly coincidental to the appearance of Jesus. This added a measure of credibility to Jesus' messianic claim. However, some partisan believers have taken things even further. Using complex calculations based on various lunar/solar calendars, they posit that Jesus entered the East Gate of Jerusalem on the exact day prescribed by scripture.

Mary's Controversial Conception

Leaping forward 438 years, it is now 6 BCE, and the setting is no longer Babylonia. Rather, we are in Roman-occupied Israel. The Hebrew people are eager for the Messiah to appear, for his predicted time is close at hand. They believe he will remove the Roman oppressors and establish the new Davidic Dynasty. Mary, the future

---

[2] Fruchtenbaum, "The Messianic Timetable According to Daniel."

mother of Jesus, resides with her parents in the trading settlement of Nazareth, approximately ninety miles north of Jerusalem.

Mary may have been in her mid-teens when she was betrothed to Joseph, who was much older. Sometime after entering their one-year period of engagement, and in the absence of Joseph, Mary became pregnant. Since she was not yet married, she was vulnerable to prosecution under Jewish law. The penalty for becoming pregnant out of wedlock was death by stoning. It did not matter whether the pregnancy occurred due to rape or was of a consensual nature. Joseph, being elsewhere at the time of conception, was upset when he returned to find his bride-to-be pregnant (Matt. 1:19).

Mary and Elizabeth: Manufacturing an Explanation

It is perhaps not surprising that early in Mary's pregnancy she was sent "with haste" to her aunt Elizabeth's house in the "hill country of Judah" (Luke 1:39). If Mary had been raped, it is conceivable she would want to leave the area to avoid the embarrassment associated with such a thing. There is also the distressing prospect that she would be "put away" if her baby had been conceived out of wedlock and the father was deemed to be someone other than her future husband. Less clear is why Mary would flee after announcing she was pregnant with the Messiah. She might well have remained in her hometown to celebrate the divine event with family and friends. Taking flight as she did is more consistent with a pregnancy that was not of divine origin. However, it is probably not fair to second-guess the situation. Fleeing would also take her out of the jurisdiction of local authorities who might want to prosecute her under Hebrew law.

In all probability, Mary and Elizabeth gave considerable thought as to how the problems associated with Mary's untimely pregnancy could be sorted out. Fortunately, the time in which she lived coincided with the prophesied appearance of the Jewish Messiah. For that reason, it must have seemed reasonable for Mary to persist with her claim that she was miraculously pregnant with the Christ. Though it presented an enormous deception, it was preferrable to being put to death or having to live out her life as the outcast mother of an illegitimate child. Mary, however, wouldn't be the only one making the claim. In that day there were many who claimed to be the Messiah. Some of those who also made the claim were:

1. Simon of Peraea
2. Athronges
3. Simon bar Kokhba
4. Simon Magus
5. Dositheos (Nathanael) the Samaritan[3]
6. Taheb, the Samaritan messiah[4]

There were many lesser-known messianic claimants, as well.

Mary and Elizabeth possibly borrowed from the story of Samson in attempting to manage the delicate situation. Significant parallels exist between the two stories. Since divine intervention had occurred previously, it might seem reasonable for Mary to claim an angel also appeared to her.

Before his conception, Samson's peasant mother, who was barren, was visited by an angel of the Lord who told her that she would bear a son who would become a Nazarite. The Nazarite sect consisted of those who were dedicated to the special service of God. The angel further foretold that her son would "deliver Israel from the hand of the Philistines" (Judg. 13). He would therefore be a type of savior. Samson typifies Hebrew saviors, who historically saved Jews from oppression instead of their sin.

Remarkably, Luke 1:36 states that Elizabeth was likewise pregnant "in her old age." This miraculous circumstance had been foretold by the angel Gabriel, as well. Finally, there was the prophetic verse in the book of Isaiah that foretold of a virgin conceiving and giving birth. Mary might have believed the sum of the correlations would support her contention that she was immaculately pregnant with the Messiah. Her fervent hope was that

---

[3] "List of Jewish Messiah Claimants."
[4] Prather, "Tahab—The Samaritan Messiah" and Barton, "The Samaritan Messiah."

the story would resonate with the Jewish community. Mary's only concern was that she needed to deliver a male baby. If not, she would at least be out of Nazareth, where condemnation would be substantial. Apart from that, the script had already been written, and it fit quite well with the circumstances Mary was facing.

Mary would tell Joseph of her "good fortune" and, after receiving assurance from yet another angel (Matt. 1:21), Joseph decided to believe her. Her story appeared to be working. However, there would be no point at which she could renege. Accordingly, Jesus would be told from early childhood that he was the Son of God as well as the Jewish Messiah.

Virgin Birth and Medical Considerations

Before proceeding further, perhaps the medical potential for virgin conception should be briefly reviewed. A data analysis published in the *British Medical Journal* (2013) found that "of 7,870 women who participated in the National Longitudinal Study of Adolescent Health, 45 women said they had a virgin pregnancy that wasn't related to reproductive assistance." To be clear, the study did not imply that no male partner was involved in these types of "virgin" births. Rather, "fooling around" is implicated. Teenage girls, whose reproductive health is at its prime, make up the preponderance of females claiming virgin birth[5].

There have been reports of human virgin births occurring without a male partner through the process of parthenogenesis. Suffice it to say that parthenogenesis never produces a viable embryo of all-maternal origin. The extremely rare process produces a viable baby (chimera) that has two cell lineages in its body. One is of biparental origin and the other results from the spontaneous activation of a single maternal oocyte.[6]

How, then, does this information apply to a discussion regarding the alleged virgin birth of Mary? For one, it means that there is no medical possibility that Mary could have produced a male

---

[5] Miller, "Can You Get Pregnant Without Having Sex?"
[6] Pianka, "Virgin Birth in Human Females?" and Strain, Warner, Johnston et al, "A human parthenogenetic chimaera," 164–169.

child through parthenogenesis. An informed probability requires that a human male partner was involved in some fashion.

Yeshua ben Pantera

Excluding the Holy Spirit, who could possibly have been the father of Jesus? Only one human male has ever been mentioned as the potential biological father of Jesus of Nazareth. What follows is the anecdotal evidence that implicates him.

An appellation in the Talmud credits a Roman archer named Pantera as having raped Mary and points a finger at him as being the biological father of Jesus. Since Jesus was born in 5 or 6 BCE., Pantera may have been sixteen or seventeen years old at the time of Jesus' birth. It is historically accurate that a young Roman soldier named Tiberius Julius Abdes Pantera (b. 22 BCE, Sidon, Phoenicia, d. 40 CE), was stationed in the northern district of Galilee at the time of Jesus' conception. Given the possible similarities in age, some consideration could be given to the idea that Mary's pregnancy was the result of a teenage tryst and not a rape. The Greek philosopher Celsus and an early Christian writer named Origen Alexandria both reported that Mary had been convicted of adultery and had a child by a certain soldier named Pantera.[7] Pantera was subsequently transferred to Germany in 9 CE to help Roman general Varus put down the Germanic tribal rebellion. Two rabbinic texts also reference *Yeshu ben Pantera* (Jesus, son of Pantera).[8]

Meanwhile, given the controversial circumstances surrounding Mary's pregnancy, it might have behooved the Jewish leadership of that time to discredit the claim that Jesus was the Messiah. Proposing that Pantera was Jesus' real father would accomplish such a thing. Some contemporary theologians have contended that the accusation was indeed made by Hebrew authorities.[9] If Pantera *was* the father of Jesus, then the ethnicity of the Christ would be a mixture of Jew and Canaanite (Gentile). With certainty, Christian critics emphatically denounce claims of Mary

---

[7] Tabor, "Who is a Jew?"
[8] Helwig-Larsen, "Jesus, Son of Pantera."
[9] Jaffe, "The Virgin Birth of Jesus in the Talmudic Context," 577–92.

becoming pregnant by an earthly father. It is their forceful assertion that the Holy Spirit fathered Jesus (Matt. 1:18–20).

At one point during his three-year ministry, Jesus traveled north from Galilee to the Mediterranean coast. His enigmatic journey was brief, and only the Gospels of Matthew and Mark (Matt. 15:21, Mark 7:24–31) mention it. His destination was the Phoenician cities of Sidon and Tyre. Strangely, Jesus entered a certain house in Sidon "and wanted no one to know it." Who was he going to see? There is no mention of what his intentions were. Could it have been a visit to meet with his father, Pantera, who was born and raised there? It is an enticing thought that carries a note of plausibility.

Hebrew Monotheism and the Holy Spirit

Whatever the cause of Mary's pregnancy, and whoever was responsible, it remained Mary's impassioned claim that the Holy Spirit fathered her child. Unfortunately for Mary, a careful review of Jewish theology exposes an important point. The Hebrew faith does not recognize the concept of the Holy Spirit. It does not exist in Judaism.

The Hebrew term for "holy spirit" is the phrase *Ruah ha-Kodesh*. Ruah means spirit, but not in the sense of an entity. The connotation it carries is similar to the concepts of ethos or essence. Ruah ha-Kodesh may also relate to divine inspiration. The first chapter of Genesis mentions "the spirit of God hovering over the face of the waters." This ethereal vision uses the Hebrew term *Ruah Elohim* (the breath or wind of God). Even though there are many mentions of the spirit of God in the *Tanakh* and other rabbinic texts, there is no mention of a Holy Spirit that corresponds to the divine singularity depicted in the New Testament. Neither is the ministry of the Holy Spirit found in the Hebrew Bible. Hebrew theology believes in only one preeminent God. That God is the Creator God, also called Yahweh. A Son of God is not part of a nonexistent *Godhead trilogy*. If there was consideration given to a Son of God, that title would apply metaphorically to King David through the promises of Psalm 2:7 and the Davidic Covenant.

The word "trinity" is not found anywhere in the Judeo-Christian Bible. The canon of the Holy Trinity was presented and argued by early church fathers at the Nicene Council in 325 CE. It is derived from Matthew 3:17, Matthew 28:19, Luke 3:22, John 14:26 and 1 John 5:7. "Trinitarianism" is viewed differently by various denominations of Christianity, including Catholicism. Judaism does not recognize the Holy Trinity.

Hebrew religious hierarchy refused to believe that Jesus was who he claimed to be. A primary reason for that rejection included that his claim to be the Son of God did not fit with Hebrew theology. Neither did they find that the Holy Spirit could have fathered Jesus, since there is no godly persona known as the Holy Spirit in Judaism.

Missing the Messianic Mark

In addition to complications brought forth by the Pantera theory and the Holy Trinity dilemma, there is another difficulty that was raised by detractors of Jesus. It centers on messianic lineage. A core condition established in Hebrew theology and its traditions mandates that the Messiah be born of the royal bloodline of King David. David is presented as being the Messiah's father through his "seed." However, Christian scholars maintain that Hebrew Bible references to the seed of David are ambiguous and not necessarily binding as regards the Messiah. Their contention is that Jesus was the legal son of Joseph by marriage, if not by birth. It is asserted that Mary was married to Joseph, and through that relationship, Jesus gained access to the House of David. Hebrew law *did* allow for an adopted son to be considered the legal son of his stepfather. This fact notwithstanding, biblical references to "seed" mean just what is implied. *Jesus could not become part of the Davidic bloodline through marriage, adoption, or association.* Just as an American president *must* be a natural-born citizen of the United States, the Hebrew Messiah *must* be a direct descendant of King David, by birth.

There are nine mentions of the "seed of David" in the Judeo-Christian Bible. Five references occur in the Protestant Old Testament. They are: 1 Kings 11:39, 1 Kings 13:2, 1 Kings 14:8, Jeremiah 33:22, and Jeremiah 33:36. Although none of these scriptures mention Jesus (Yeshua), some use the term Christ, which is Greek for Messiah. Four New Testament verses use "seed of David" within the text. The verses—John 7:42, Romans 1:3, Romans 1:4, and 2 Timothy 2:8—are not prophetic, but are instead misleading while attempting to connect the Son of God and Jesus Christ with the term "seed of David."

The books of Matthew and Luke both describe alleged genealogies from David to Jesus. They differ in that one is maternal and the other is paternal. Luke records that the Davidic bloodline for Jesus ends with his mother, Mary. Jewish law derived from the Torah declares that tribal lineages *only* pass from father to son and not to daughters. Mary's father (Joachim) could only pass his tribal lineage to his sons. When a daughter is born to a given tribe, if she marries, her tribe becomes that of her husband. Her children inherit her husband's tribe but only in rare instances where they are his own biological children. Lineage in the tribe of Judah (Kings) only passes from a father to his biological son.

Genetics and Davidic Lineage

Genetic science has recently been invoked in an effort to settle longstanding disputes surrounding the lineage of King David. It has been said that the DNA does not lie. Jewish truth seekers, the curious, and others eagerly await the results of genetic analysis. Investigations include an ongoing effort to establish a composite Hebrew family tree. This undertaking has involved massive amounts of research and has created a monumental database. Much like the Mormons, Jewish geneticists and genealogists are seeking to fix inheritance for every Jew who has ever lived. Research has already established the lineage of Aaron, brother of Moses. Y Chromosome Aaron, otherwise known as the Cohen Modal Haplotype, represents the Jewish priestly line (the Cohanim).[10] In all, there are at least a dozen independent programs working to establish one or more ethnicities or lineages. DavidicDynasty.org is attempting to define the truthful lineage of King David. Of even

---

[10] Behar and Hammer, "Extended Y chromosome haplotypes."

greater potential importance, questions surrounding Jesus of Nazareth may ultimately be answered via genetic investigation.

Religious scoffers who disdain science cannot dispute the faith-based notion that God clearly understands genetics. It follows that he would know the importance of the Y chromosome. A long-understood genetic fact has disclosed that human males possess an XY pairing of chromosomes, while females possess an XX pairing on the sex (gender) chromosome. A genetic segment carried on the Y chromosome delivers the male determination gene. Since Hebrew lineage is passed along an all-male line, it follows that the Y chromosome must play a defining role in Jewish lineage. Once a female X chromosome replaces a male Y chromosome, male lineage is lost. Mary's procreation partner (the father of Jesus) would have needed to donate the Y chromosome that delivered the maleness of Jesus. Mary did not receive it from her own father, whose X chromosome from his XY pair was the donated DNA strand. Thus, her alleged Davidic lineage through David's son, Nathan, was lost. Further, if Jesus was fathered by the Holy Spirit, either he was a haploid individual (incompatible with life) or the Holy Spirit is a corporeal being, capable of genetic reproduction.

The Blood Curse of Jeconiah

Most Christians are not familiar with the blood curse of Jeconiah. It is not widely taught, even though it is scripturally valid and relevant. Arguments refuting it are problematic and weak. This little-known narrative remains a critical obstacle for those who believe that the Davidic bloodline extends to Joseph.

Matthew 1:12 places King Jeconiah, who ruled Judah briefly in 598 BCE, in the bloodline of King David. Therefore, Bible scholars maintain that Jesus would be a descendant of Jeconiah. However, God cursed Jeconiah as recorded in Jeremiah 22:24 and Jeremiah 22:30. God said that none of Jeconiah's offspring would prosper and that none would sit on the throne of David. This would preclude any descendant of Jeconiah from being the Messiah, Jesus included. The curse also said that Jeconiah would not prosper in his lifetime. In fact, Jeconiah and his children did prosper in his lifetime. His grandson, Zerubbabel, found favor with God and was chosen to be a ruler (but not king). Even though God declared the curse, it is concluded by Christian theologians that the curse *must* have been reversed after Jeconiah repented. How else to explain that Jeconiah prospered? Although circumstances surrounding Jeconiah's renewed prosperity seemingly imply otherwise, it is *never* stated in the Hebrew Bible that God reversed the curse. It would require direct and convincing evidence to convey that God would go back on his word. Such a thing would demonstrate that God's words are insincere, ineffectual, and unreliable. Most Hebrew scholars believe God's words "As surely as I live, declares the Lord" were compelling, and that the curse was not reversed or revised. Those who believe that the curse was reversed are of the opinion that this somehow kept Jesus in the Davidic bloodline. This is flawed thinking, as Jesus was never there in the first place. Jesus had no biological relationship with David, Jeconiah, or Joseph. Period. If Jesus had been the natural-born son of Joseph, he would have been barred from sitting on the throne of David by virtue of the curse of Jeconiah. Joseph was banned from conveying or conferring anything to Jesus or anyone. Hence, the blood curse of Jeconiah offers a secondary reason establishing that Jesus could not be the Messiah. Today's Jewish community refutes the spurious explanations invented by Christianity. They continue to wait for their Messiah and expect him to be of the seed of David and the tribe of Judah.

***

Commentary

What have we learned from Chapter One? What can be said regarding the early storyline of Jesus?

We know that the time was right for the appearance of the Hebrew Messiah and that Mary may have taken advantage of that fact and used it to her benefit. We know it is plausible that Mary then used other correlating information, gleaned from the *Tanakh*, in creating a story designed to protect her from legal prosecution and the wrath of her betrothed.

Further, we can say with certainty there are several issues that would prevent Jesus from achieving status as the Messiah. For one, Mary's contention that she was immaculately impregnated by the Holy Spirit is contrary to Hebrew theology. The Holy Spirit does not exist in Judaism. Additionally, as we will discover later, the virgin birth prophecy described in Isaiah 7:14 is specious, at least with respect to a distant-future virgin birth. And of the greatest importance is the fact that Jesus did not come from the lineage of King David. Even genetic considerations support that he could not have. And lastly, we now understand that Jesus unabashedly took from David in proclaiming himself to be the Son of God. David's place as the Son of God was guaranteed through the promises God made in the Davidic Covenant, and as expressed in Psalm 2:7.

So, where do we go from here? The next chapter, "The Birth of Jesus," covers most of the events prior to and immediately following the nativity and, of course, the nativity itself. We will challenge much of what was written about the nativity using the Bible's own words. We will closely examine a significant finding that may overturn everything you thought you knew about the birth of Jesus.

In addition, please continue to consider the evidence. What impact might it have with respect to any future decisions you make about your relationship with Jesus? If Christianity has not been working for you, it may be because the story of Jesus is not founded on truth.

2

The Birth of Jesus

In this chapter, we will continue to examine the circumstances and events that surrounded the early life of Jesus. The biblical record will continue to be our primary reference. Adjunctive information will be forthcoming from alternative sources.

Bethlehem

The prophesied birthplace of the Messiah is not quite as significant as some of the other messianic prerequisites, but it remains a conundrum, nonetheless. A prophecy found in Micah 5:2 declares that the birthplace of a future *ruler of Israel* would be in Bethlehem Ephrathah. Although there are differences of opinion among scholars regarding the exact location of this site, there is a consensus that Bethlehem of Judea best satisfies the prophecy. However, there is anecdotal evidence that may challenge that conclusion. Changes made to the original wording of Micah 5:2 also contribute to a skewed understanding of what the prophet meant and where Bethlehem truly was.

The future ruler of Israel mentioned in Micah 5 is believed to be the Messiah. However, that is not a straightforward determination. It could easily be someone else. Consider that the Old Testament differs from the Hebrew Bible on this point. The original Hebrew text was changed by New Testament authors so that the verse would be consistent with a messianic Jesus. Matthew 2:6 is a case in point. There, Matthew changes Bethlehem *Ephrathah* to Bethlehem, *in the land of Judah*. The word *clans* (plural) in the original was likewise changed by Matthew to *ruler*. *Micah 5:2 is the only verse in the Hebrew Bible that proclaims Bethlehem as the birthplace of the Messiah.* Because of that, it is a pivotal verse. Apparently, Matthew and others did not feel God's words are stringently immutable. Otherwise, they would not have changed them to suit their agenda.

If Bethlehem of Judea was indeed the true birthplace of Jesus, then we know the trip from Nazareth covered roughly ninety miles. Incredibly, it was made when Mary was at full term in her pregnancy. She delivered as soon as they arrived in Bethlehem. The journey covered miles of rugged terrain and rock-strewn roadway known as the Way of the Patriarchs. Tradition suggests that Mary rode a donkey most of the way. There is no mention of a donkey in scripture, however, so she probably walked. Whatever the mode of transportation, the route was harrowing and punishing. The journey would have taken five to seven days to accomplish. A few who have attempted to mimic the trip describe it as being too grueling for a woman in an advanced pregnancy. So, how did Joseph and Mary do it? Maybe they did not.

Seven miles northwest of Nazareth lies the small farming village known as Bethlehem…of Galilee. Archaeologists who have excavated there believe ample evidence exists to support that *this* Bethlehem is the one where Jesus was born.[1] Many artifacts dating to the first century have been uncovered during excavations. At that time, a fortification wall, built by Justinian, surrounded the town. Remnants of it still circle the village today. A large, ornate church, now suspiciously re-buried and covered by a paved road, yields evidence that the site was built to celebrate the birthplace of the Christ. Mary and Joseph would have experienced little trouble traveling the short distance from Nazareth to Bethlehem of Galilee. But for a single prophetic verse, and certain scriptural augmentations, this common-sense venue for the birthplace of Jesus sits unrecognized, quietly tucked away among the soft rolling hills of Galilee.

The Nativity Story

Things begin to get more serious at this juncture. What comes next is very significant. That Christianity has looked past it is indefensible.

---

[1] Frenkel, "Dig Finds Evidence of Another Bethlehem."

The Bible reports that the time when Jesus was to be born coincided with the Roman census of Cyrenius. Mary and Joseph were required to travel to Bethlehem of Judea for the purpose of participating in the census. Bethlehem was the city of David, and, of course, a prophecy foretold that the Messiah would be born there. The account of the birth of Jesus given in Luke begins in chapter two: "And it came to pass in those days that a decree went out from Caesar Augustus that all the world should be registered. This census took place while Cyrenius was governor over Syria."

The census of Cyrenius (also known as Quirinius) took place upon the imposition of direct Roman rule in 6 CE.[2] Cyrenius had been placed as legate governor after Herod the Great's son, Herod Archelaus, proved to be an even worse tyrant than his father and was removed from office. Herod the Great died in 4 BCE. Archelaus was banished from office in 6 CE. Therefore, the account in Luke is erroneous when compared against historical facts. Herod had been dead for ten years at the time of the first Roman census. Cyrenius was not governor until at least twelve years after the birth of Jesus.[3]

The implications of this biblical error are critically important in that they set the entire birth-of-Christ scenario on its ear. If the census of Cyrenius took place twelve years after the birth of Jesus, then the holy family was not in Bethlehem of Judea at the time he was born. Their reason for being there was nonexistent. This enhances the likelihood that Jesus was born in Nazareth or, perhaps, Bethlehem of Galilee.

Some might suggest that the holy family came to Bethlehem nonetheless, even though there was no apparent reason for them to do so. Of course, this ignores that Mary's condition would have made an elective trip problematic, if not downright dangerous. It was the Roman census that forced them to make an ill-advised trip. The family returned home to Nazareth in Luke's account, thereby removing them from Herod's reach. However, Luke does not speak of an infant massacre or of an escape to Egypt. The Herod storylines do not happen in Luke's account.

---

[2] "Census of Quirinius."
[3] "Quirinius."

Besides being another indication that biblical inerrancy is a flawed doctrine, this evidence casts doubt on the Jesus narrative at many levels. For one, it implies that Luke was not the author of the book that bears his name. Certainly, it shores up the opinions of those who believe the Gospels were written by others in the late first century and beyond—writers who were not clear on the historical record. We are left wondering exactly where Jesus was born. More importantly, it must be asked: how far-reaching are the irregularities? For the sake of continued investigation, judgment will be withheld until all the evidence is in. We will push on as if Luke's account is accurate.

The Magi

Far away, possibly in Persia, the Magi were said to have seen *the rising of a star in the east*, which told them of the birth of a king in the west. The Magi prepared to travel west and pay homage to the newborn king. They were most likely Chaldean or Zoroastrian priests. Another theory is that they were mystics from a far-off land, possibly China.[4] Interestingly, the Greek word *magos* (magic) appears in both the Old and New Testaments. Everywhere it occurs, except in the Gospel of Matthew, it is translated *magician* or *sorcerer* in the vein of an illusionist. Where the word relates to the birth of Jesus, the translators used *wise men* instead.[5]

The Bible mentions three gifts that the Magi brought to Jesus: gold, frankincense, and myrrh. The number of gifts does not necessarily indicate that each Magus brought one gift and that there were therefore three of them. The distance they traveled was great, and it can be assumed that there was a large entourage of Magi that included attendants, ancillary personnel, and possibly even security troops. There were likely dozens of people who made the journey, including more than just a few Magi. Christmas nativity scenes typically picture three wise men gathered at the manger where Jesus was born. In truth, there were many wise men, and they were not present when Jesus was born, or any time soon afterward (if ever).

---

[4] Landau, "Who Were the Magi?"
[5] Amirault, "The Christ Child and the Wise Men."

Depending on where the journey began, estimates suggest it would have taken about two years for the caravan to arrive in Judea. It was for that reason Herod allegedly ordered that all males under two years of age be killed. Known as the Massacre of the Innocents, Herod's order came after the Magi inquired about the new king and where he could be found.[6] Since Herod's advisors knew of the messianic connection to Bethlehem, Herod would already have known where the new king would be. Clearly, the Magi were pointed toward Bethlehem by someone. They then failed to return and pass the whereabouts of Jesus on to Herod, as he had requested.

According to Matthew, the star of Bethlehem directed the Magi from Jerusalem to the nearby town of Bethlehem. The text implies the star was mobile and that it traveled the six miles to Bethlehem ahead of the caravan. Obviously, it would be impossible for a heavenly body to move six miles from its position and be detected from millions of miles away. That it then hovered directly over a given home is a fanciful tale. Further, Matthew's account implies that only the Magi saw the star, so there is considerable room for skepticism.

Herod had been crowned King of the Jews by the Roman Senate in 40 BCE. Although Herod was known to have become paranoid in his later years, it seems unlikely he would have felt a two-year-old child posed a threat to his throne. He was old and infirm at the time of this occurrence and died shortly thereafter. Thankfully, there is little or no merit to the story of the massacre.[7]

Bethlehem of Judea was a small town of about 1,500 residents in the time of Herod the Great. Estimates are that only a dozen male toddlers under the age of two were living there when the alleged slaughter occurred. Certainly, it was not justified to murder a dozen or more babies under the circumstances. There is nothing in the historical record that tells of such a slaughter. Not that Herod had been above committing atrocities. It is likely that Matthew borrowed from another infanticide event that allegedly occurred in Rome in 63 BCE. In that day, Magi are believed to have traveled to Rome and appeared before the Senate to tell them that a ruler had

---

[6] McGrath, "Am I Wrong About the Massacre of the Innocents?"
[7] "Massacre of the Innocents."

been born according to a celestial prophecy. The news of a potential new ruler was unsettling to the Senate, and a decree went out to kill all young males in the candidate range. Rome was notorious for infanticide. It is therefore quite possible that this event, if true, may be the inspiration behind Matthew's decision to include such a story in his own version of the birth of Jesus.

Another hypothetical that may explain the origins of the Bethlehem infanticide story comes from Exodus 1:22: "And the Pharaoh charged all his people, saying, 'Every son that is born ye shall cast into the river, and every daughter ye shall save alive.'" The Pharaoh ordered the deaths of all young Jewish males after being warned by Egyptian scribes of a Jewish threat to his rule. Bible scholars tend to support this allegory, especially after considering embellishments that were incorporated up until the first century.[8]

Further chipping away at Matthew's credibility is his flawed interpretation of a prophecy from Jeremiah 31:15. While attempting to draw prophetic parallels to his massacre report, Matthew ignored context and twisted the truth. The event in question refers to a time when the Assyrians brutally invaded Ramah in ancient Israel and killed many, including children. Even Bible scholars are baffled by Matthew's lack of understanding regarding the passage. In all probability, he did understand it but chose to use a false interpretation to suit his purposes.

Matthew's unprincipled pen continues to abet his agenda by claiming that Joseph and Mary fled to Egypt after Joseph had a dream warning him that Herod was a threat. Jesus would have been approximately two years old at the time. The Magi supposedly found the family living in a house in Bethlehem. It appears Matthew believed they had remained in the area since Jesus was born. Otherwise, Matthew may be proposing that they were in Bethlehem, and not Nazareth, all along (see below). Luke, of course, wrote that the holy family stayed in Jerusalem for forty days and then returned to Nazareth. Even though it promotes confusion, it was thoughtful of Matthew and Luke to give us a choice.

Adding to the uncertainty is Matthew's discourse (Matt. 2:20–23) describing the return of the family from Egypt after Herod

---

[8] "Massacre of the Innocents."

the Great died. Matthew states that when Joseph heard Herod Archelaus was on the throne in Judea, "he was afraid to go there." For that reason, "he turned aside into the region of Galilee" where they "dwelt in a city called Nazareth." Clearly, Matthew believed that Joseph was restrained from returning home to Bethlehem and was compelled by this circumstance to dwell in Nazareth instead. His account strongly implies that the family had never resided in Galilee previously. Nor does his account place Mary in Nazareth prior to the birth of Jesus.

In fact, Jesus did grow up in Nazareth, but there remain unresolved contradictions with respect to what happened during the few years immediately following his birth. Whether or not the holy family went to Egypt at some point is left to speculation, as there is no historical evidence to indicate they did. Some Bible scholars believe Matthew included the story in order to satisfy a prophecy found in Hosea 11:1. That prophecy suggested, according to Matthew at least, that the Messiah would come out of Egypt. Hosea 11:1 is not a messianic prophecy, however, but relates instead to the Exodus. Coptic Christians in Ethiopia and Egypt steadfastly believe that Jesus was in northeastern Egypt for several years. There is, indeed, a deep connection between Christianity and the Egyptian Copts because of this.

What's in a Name?

As we already know, the biblical account tells that Mary was visited by the angel Gabriel, who advised her that she would conceive a child by the Holy Spirit. Further, she was informed that her child would be the "Son of God" and that she should call him "Jesus" (Luke 1:31). When searching out the connotation of the name Jesus (Yeshua), a variety of meanings and phrases come to light. Among them are God Saves, Messiah, Anointed One, and God is Salvation.

In the Protestant Old Testament book of Isaiah, an angel foretells that a child would be born of a virgin (see Chapter 12). This male child would be named Immanuel (God with us). Christians cite Matthew 1:22–23 when attempting to connect Isaiah 7:14 prophetically to the birth of Jesus. It is somewhat befuddling that Mary would be instructed to name her baby Jesus and not Immanuel.

However, it does stand to reason, in that Isaiah 7:14 is not a messianic prophecy and does not pertain to Jesus of Nazareth.

Another passage from Isaiah that is not dissimilar, at least with respect to its erroneous interpretation, is one which was later adapted into a popular Christmas song. Like Isaiah 7:14, it is not prophetic about the birth of Jesus, either. It is prophetic about King Hezekiah. Isaiah 9:6–7, verse 6 reads in part: "For unto us a child is born, unto is a son is given; and the government shall be upon his shoulder. And his name will be called Wonderful, Counselor, Mighty God, Everlasting Father, Prince of Peace." Verse 7: "Of the increase of his government and peace, there will be no end."

The Hebrew name Hezekiah means Mighty God, and Judaic theology instructs that this predicts how God will demonstrate his power through the life of King Hezekiah. As was the case with Immanuel, this prophecy was also fulfilled, but not by Jesus. Christian apologists claim that Jesus is mentioned throughout their Old Testament. In reality, the name Yeshua (Jesus) is never mentioned in the Hebrew Bible. The Judeo-Christian Old Testament uses appellative trickery to create the illusion that Jesus is found throughout its pages. For instance, even though the word "Salvation" appears more than 150 times in the Old Testament, in most instances, it was originally used as a common noun (salvation) and not as a proper noun. Hermeneutic etymologists falsely assert that Jesus is mentioned indirectly whenever an Old Testament reference is made to Salvation, God Saves, etc. They should know it is a grammatical breach to convert common nouns in such an appellative manner. An even more egregious breach occurs when some Bible scholars advance the spurious idea that capitalization of descriptive names is not even necessary for identifying Jesus. Their exegetical interpretations allow them to cite his name anywhere they choose. The obvious questions arise: Why was the name Yeshua not used directly in the Hebrew Bible when prophetically referencing Jesus? If the intention was to highlight the future Messiah, why would Hebrew scribes be so cryptic?

Descriptive phrases used in conjunction with Hebrew names are not normally meant to define an individual but are essentially aggrandizing pseudonyms. Jesus was an extremely common name for boys in the first century. Hence, the descriptive meanings assessed to Jesus of Nazareth should not be applied solely to him to the exclusion of all other boys named Jesus. There were, no doubt, many boys named Jesus who were born in Bethlehem and who were of true Davidic lineage. Apparently, none of them took it upon themselves to lay claim to being the Messiah. They knew they were not, even if Jesus of Nazareth did not.

Growing Up

The life of Jesus as a child is not well documented, even in the Bible. There is a reference to his being in the Temple in Jerusalem at age twelve and that his family regularly traveled to Jerusalem at Passover. Apparently, on one occasion Jesus stayed behind on the return trip to Nazareth. His parents, who thought he might be with friends, were unaware that he was still in Jerusalem. It took them three days to find him after they realized he was missing. They found him in the Temple, "sitting in the midst of the teachers, both listening to them and asking them questions." Verse 47 of Luke 2 says, "And all who heard him were astonished at his understanding and answers." Then followed an interesting exchange between Jesus and his parents. When admonished for staying behind, Jesus responded by saying, "Why did you seek me? Did you not know that I must be about my Father's business?" According to Luke 2:50, they failed to understand what he had said to them. How is that so? His parents surely knew that they were raising the Son of God. In that context, it should have made perfect sense to them.

As an adolescent, Jesus spent countless hours in synagogues and the Temple. He spent his time there learning God's Word and eventually (years later) teaching it. Jesus came to know well the messianic prophecies contained in the Hebrew Bible, and he would set out to fulfill as many of them as he could. In all, Jesus was able to satisfy about 100 prophecies, although some have claimed it was perhaps as many as 350[9]. He was able to fulfill many of them, but not all. It is important to note here, that if someone already knows what the prophecies are, it is simply a matter of time, effort, and

---

[9] "44 Prophecies Jesus Christ Fulfilled" and "351 Old Testament Prophecies."

logistics to see that they are accomplished. Biblical scholars sometimes speak of the mathematical probabilities involved with the satisfaction of prophecies by Jesus. Those mathematical determinations should only apply if the prophecies are *not* known to the one that satisfies them. That would be *truly* miraculous! What Jesus did was not necessarily so extraordinary. Over and over, it is written that Jesus accomplished something "that it might be fulfilled." Matthew 5:17 records Jesus as saying, "Do not think that I have come to abolish the Law or the Prophets; I have not come to abolish them but to fulfill them." For him, satisfying Hebrew law and fulfilling the words of the prophets was the centerpiece of his ministry.

As Jesus grew, he learned the trade of carpentry. Both he and his stepfather, Joseph, were known to be carpenters. It is possible that they worked together in nearby Sepphoris, which was undergoing rapid expansion as the Roman capital of the Galilee province. Nazareth was a suburb of Sepphoris, which was an hour's commute by foot. Jesus may have worked there for many years before starting his ministry at age thirty. However, rumors persist that Jesus was in the east learning magic during this blacked-out period. There are eighteen years where no written record exists regarding his activities or his whereabouts.

***

Commentary

The complexities of Chapter Two may generate a few headaches. The differing accounts may present readers with a little too much confusion. Attempting to sort out the true story from conflicting accounts is an exercise in frustration.

It appears that Matthew's account is forged from his desire to satisfy prophecy. It has the ring of a fictional script. It was written primarily to connect prophetic dots. He does seem to draw frequent parallels between Moses and Jesus while faithfully attempting to link the two prophetically. Those efforts are too conspicuous to allow for credibility.

Luke's story is somewhat different. It fails to accurately report on historic events which are pertinent to the Jesus backstory. Such a thing yields the appearance that his report is flawed. When considering the importance of the birth of Jesus, it is unsettling that the story could not be accurately told.

The book of Mark does not involve itself with the birth and early life of Jesus. Mark's narrative begins with the ministry of Jesus. The apostle John likewise fails to mention anything about the early life of Jesus. He may have felt it unimportant in light of the bigger picture. Since he and Jesus were cousins, it can be assumed that they thoroughly knew each other's history.

Wide-ranging testimony subverts the credibility of the narrative. After all, we are supposedly talking about the Word of God. Said to be inerrant and completely truthful, these conflicting accounts severely undermine that contention. The inconsistencies should not be glossed over or dismissed. In a circumstance where the lives of countless human beings are impacted over long spans of time, it is of the utmost importance that reports and accounts are consistent, so that truth prevails and no doubt remains.

Gathering Followers

The public ministry of Jesus began when his cousin, John the Baptist, immersed him into the Jordan River and baptized him. John did not feel worthy to baptize Jesus and thought it should instead be Jesus who baptized him. Jesus told John it was "fitting for us to fulfill all righteousness," so John proceeded to baptize him.

Following his baptism, Jesus went into the Judean wilderness to pray and fast for forty days. The Gospel of Luke recounts that he was tempted by Satan for the entirety of his time there (Luke 4:1–2). Satan challenged Jesus to do a number of things in order to prove he was the Son of God. Jesus did none of these things. Instead, he rebuked Satan, who eventually departed. It is not clear why he would submit to taunting and questioning for forty days, unless it was a test that he willingly participated in.

The number forty is mentioned one hundred and forty-six times throughout the Bible. Like Jesus, Moses and Elijah each fasted for forty days (1 Kings 19:7–8, Deut. 9:9). Fasting in these instances meant abstaining from food and water. Water would have been hard for Jesus to come by in the parched Judean desert. An individual in good condition can go without food and water for about a week. With water, death becomes imminent somewhere around six weeks. However, being in an arid environment would expedite dehydration and substantially lessen the survivable duration of a fast. Thus, the accounts of these fasts represent baseless claims that are physiologically impossible.

Jesus' original intention in going to the wilderness might simply have been to clear his mind and prepare for his ministry. Psychiatrist and author Anthony Storr notes that "Jesus was going through a period of internal conflict during his time of fasting in the desert."[1] What was the nature of the conflict? Was Jesus having doubts? The Bible does not elaborate on this. The overall impression one gets is that this time of testing was emotionally and mentally intense. It would have also been physically draining, if not fatal.

After this time alone in the wilderness, Jesus went to Galilee to begin his ministry of preaching, teaching, and healing. Luke 4:16 says: "Then He came to Nazareth, where He had been brought up. And as His custom was, He went into the synagogue on the Sabbath Day, and stood up to read." Jesus was given the book of Isaiah to read from. He read a passage that referred, he believed, to himself. Part of the passage (Isa. 61:1–2) reads as follows: "He has anointed me to preach the gospel to the poor; He has sent me to heal the brokenhearted, to proclaim liberty to the captives and recover sight to the blind."

Completing his reading, Jesus proclaimed, "Today this scripture is fulfilled in your hearing," meaning that he was the one he had just read about. As the passage proceeded, Jesus began to make arrogant and disparaging comments with respect to the prophet Elijah. These comments were not well received. Luke 4:28 says: "All those in the synagogue, when they heard these things, were filled with wrath." The congregation rose up and ran Jesus out of the city to a place where there was a cliff and attempted to throw him over it. Thus, the first act of Jesus' ministry led to a mob attempt on his life. Luckily for Jesus, he was able to get past the crowd and escape. This may well have been a preview of things to come.

There was no subtlety in Jesus. He did not hesitate to make statements that are recorded as being offensive and insensitive. He spoke with authority in a style that was bold and unapologetic. He sometimes appeared to lack discernment, and he did not mind insulting the beliefs of those he spoke to. At other times, it seemed like Jesus talked down to people. The fact that he often spoke in parables would imply that he did not think his audiences could understand him if he spoke directly. This occasionally conveyed the appearance that he was aloof. Hence, he was not always liked or highly esteemed. Many who enthusiastically followed him at first, eventually dropped off:

---

[1] Storr, *Feet of Clay*.

> John 6:66: From that time many of His disciples went back and walked with Him no more.
>
> John 10:20: Many of them said, He has a devil, and is mad; why listen to Him?

After his close call in Nazareth, Jesus set out to continue his ministry in Galilee. Almost immediately he began to gather followers. He found the original twelve disciples in various places. Although their names are known, the Bible does not describe all their backgrounds. We only know that four were fishermen and one was a tax collector. Early on, Jesus challenged the new group of twelve with the following words: "If anyone desires to come after me, let him deny himself, and take up his cross, and follow me" (Matt. 16:24). What did that mean?

Undivided Devotion

To take up one's cross was an expression that related to the day in which Jesus lived. Those who were condemned to crucifixion were made to *take up their cross* and carry it to the place where the crucifixion would occur. In the context that Jesus meant it, he was telling them they would have to crucify themselves before they could follow him. That was an allegorical way of saying they would have to come to the end of who they were and submit themselves totally to Jesus and his cause. Their own will would have to be subordinated to his will. Evangelical preachers faithfully challenge followers of Jesus with this even now. To highlight this requirement for total and unwavering devotion, Jesus would make an extraordinary statement in Luke 14:26 when speaking to "a great multitude":

> If anyone comes to me and does not hate [his] father and mother, wife and children, brothers and sisters, yes, even their own life, such a person cannot be my disciple.

It is puzzling why Jesus would make such a paradoxical statement. It conveyed the impression that he was directing his followers to defy the commandments to "love one another" and to "honor your father and mother." This appeal asked for a level of devotion that would result in a violation of scripture. It seemingly implies he was asking his followers to commit sin. The original Greek word used in this text is *miseo,* which means "to hate, despise, or revile".

Jesus wittingly placed his followers in a moral and spiritual dilemma. When Christians are asked to elaborate on this, their response is not consistent with a literal interpretation. Instead, a qualification is presented explaining that followers need to *put Jesus first in all matters*, including family matters. But of course, that is not what this specific text is saying. The Greek word *miseo* means "hate" in every sense of the word. It is not open to interpretation unless it is ascribed to some measure of hyperbole.

In a final attempt to reconcile this predicament, reference is made to the doctrine of biblical inerrancy. We are asked to *trust* there is a reason this illustration has been used. There is no apparent resolution in the matter. The paradox is simply dispatched by revising the text or invoking a mitigating doctrine. Many biblical contradictions are dealt with in the same manner.

Luke 9:59–62 underscores that the passage above is not hyperbole. Instead, it reflects that Jesus could be callous, even when responding to some who eagerly desired to follow him:

> Then He said to another [who desired to follow him], 'Follow Me.' But he said, 'Lord let me first go and bury my father.' Jesus said to him, 'Let the dead bury their own, but you go and preach the Kingdom of God.' And another said, 'Lord, I will follow You, but let me first go and bid farewell to my family.' But Jesus said to him, 'No one, having put his hand to the plow, and looking back, is fit for the Kingdom of God.

The sentiment expressed in these verses highlights an insensitive and unreasonable Jesus. These encounters speak for themselves. It is uncommon to hear any expository on them in a church, for they depict a Jesus that is very different than the one typically presented.

More on the Family

Although many subscribe to the view that God created and ordained the family (Gen. 2:24), Jesus was known for sometimes preaching in contradiction to that. And, in spite of conjecture that Jesus was married and may even have had a son, he occasionally spoke out against wedlock, as well. When he commissioned and sent forth his newly gathered disciples, he directed them to advance certain messages, including the following:

> The sons of this age marry and are given in marriage. But they who shall be accounted worthy to obtain that world, and the resurrection from the dead, neither marry, nor are given in marriage (Luke 20:35).

> I am come to set a man at variance against his father, and the daughter against her mother, and the daughter-in-law against her mother-in-law. And a man's foes shall be they of his own household (Matt. 10:35–36).

Perceptive inquisitors have wondered, "Was Jesus committed to destroying marriage and family?" People regularly speak of biblical contradictions. This is one. Where God commanded in Genesis 2:24 that a man should leave his parents and hold fast to his wife, Jesus sought to tear the entire institution apart for selfish reasons. Ask yourself, what would be your reaction to the message of Jesus at this point? Would you turn and walk away? Or would you willingly surrender your life, then leave your family behind, out of devotion to him?

"Follow Me"

At this stage of his ministry, Jesus insisted on complete loyalty and submission to himself and his cause. The biblical record establishes that he did not want families or married couples in his movement. He only sought slave-like devotion from individuals who were singularly fixed on him. There have been many guru-type leaders who have sought to control vulnerable groups of people. Indeed, many lost souls do leave their families to follow controlling leaders. These gullible, and often needy, individuals readily embrace the cult's maladjusted teachings. Jim Jones, David Koresh, and Bhagwan Shree Rajneesh are only a few of the many cult leaders who have used the power of belief to influence and manipulate desperate followers. These purveyors of woe often engaged in preaching doomsday prophecies. Like them, Jesus preached fear-based messages of apocalypse where only he could offer a path to salvation. He brashly offered himself up as their only hope. For cynics who view Jesus with a jaundiced eye, it is perturbing that he and those who followed built, and have managed to sustain, a worldwide religious movement that has beguiled millions upon millions for two thousand years.

Hometown Repudiation

It was inevitable that Jesus would take his message home to Nazareth. Would he be welcomed? Not so much.
John 7:5 reveals: "Even his own brothers did not believe in him." Likewise, others who had long known Jesus also rejected the righteous prophet he was professing himself to be. They believed his new persona was self-imposed. The Gospels record the following dialogues:

> When Jesus had come into his own country, He taught them in their synagogue, so that they were surprised and said, 'Where did this man get his wisdom ... is this not the carpenter's son? Is not his mother called Mary? And are not His brothers and sisters here with us?' So they were offended by Him. (Matt. 13:55–57 and Mark 6:2–4).

and

> Is this not Jesus, the son of Joseph, whose father and mother we know? How is it then that he saith, I came down from heaven? (John 6:42)

Clearly, Jesus failed to gain favorable recognition in his homeland. He was seen as a typical Galilean—a man who had never demonstrated that he was special or extraordinary. He proudly returned to preach to those who had known him since childhood. But alas, they were offended that he was suddenly projecting himself as a prophet. They readily saw through his pretense. To them, he was a carpenter and nothing more. Indeed, Jesus said: "No prophet is accepted in his own country" (Luke 4:24).

The reason behind this relates directly to the fact that one's hometown peers know your history. If Jesus had been raised as the Son of God, how can it be that his friends, and even his siblings, did not accept his newfound image? It is telling that his former companions reacted this way.

The Modern Follower of Jesus

Vast numbers of people in today's world have chosen to believe in the message of Jesus. For many, the depth of sincerity involved falls far short of the extraordinary commitment that he demands. The Bible makes it clear that Jesus does not want lukewarm dedication (Rev. 3:15–16). Nevertheless, there is often little will on the part of believers to live truly Christ-centered lives. Accordingly, many today are criticized for being casual Christians. They often straddle a spiritual line, feeling that salvation is free and the commitment part is optional. Going to church on Sunday is all that is necessary for them to connect with their lackluster faith. When church is over, they walk out the door and resume their self-focused lives.

Meanwhile, at the opposite end of the spectrum are radicalized Christians whose beliefs border on cultism. Sects such as the dominionists, as well as zealots known as Quiverfull, have embraced new and potentially dangerous concepts of the Christian walk. Standing behind Genesis 1:26, where God gave humans dominion over all the earth, dominionism makes up a theocratic movement that seeks to control the world and enforce theonomy (the Law of God). These Christian radicals oppose separation of church and state, but only for the reason of achieving a totally Bible-based government. The Quiverfull movement, consisting mostly of fundamentalist Christian couples, claims the 127th Psalm as their banner verse. The Bible-based belief that children are a God-given blessing leads members of this Christian subgroup to toss birth control and have as many children as they possibly can. The group's ultimate motives have been called into question by some. However, many others find them peculiar but harmless.

Christianity also incorporates a deeply committed group of conservative evangelicals who are staunch and rigid in their beliefs. They are sometimes said to be legalistic as they place emphasis on Christian Old Testament law. These believers cling tenaciously to the doctrines of biblical inerrancy and scriptural authority. Enter fundamentalists. Fundamentalism is not a distinct church denomination. Rather, its philosophy crosses denominational barriers. Baptists, Pentecostals, Covenant churches, Assembly of God churches, and even some branches of Presbyterianism may all be fundamental in their theology and doctrinal positions. In reality, any Bible-believing church may apply the scriptures in ways that are consistent with a strictly literal (fundamental) interpretation of the Bible. While the Statements of Faith that these churches expound may focus their emphasis on different areas of Bible ideology, they all hold a hard line on most biblical matters.

It would be unfair to accuse all Christians of being extreme in one direction or another. To be sure, many believers experience a better life as a result of their faith. It is that faith that somehow gets them through tough times and gives hope, however fanciful, for the future. These are people from all walks of life whose religious ideology helps to fill needs that might otherwise go unmet. In this case, we can offer that "what works for some, does not work for others."

One unfortunate scenario finds a cohort of devotees feeling like failures. They have become discouraged and feel spiritually outcast. Unrelenting letdowns and futile circumstances have led to exhaustion and frustration. At some point, a tragic loss may cause them to conclude they can no longer keep the faith. Many who are disillusioned will eventually walk away, wishing to rid themselves of something they find so dispiritingly dubious. *These suffering souls possess a strong resolve to stop believing in an unreliable God who has not produced results in their lives.*

***

Commentary

A few things stand out with respect to the early ministry of Jesus. First, his forty days in the wilderness was a time of reflection, planning, and preparation. It was a time of intense internal struggle, as well. However, the time that he allegedly went without food and water was not survivable. He left the desert in possession of a plan that included his involvement with close supporters, or disciples. The text is not clear how he hoped to use them. Would he use them as advisors, scouts, emissaries, or all of the above?

With the exception of Peter, the group Jesus chose probably consisted entirely of bachelors. There is some indication they were all under eighteen years old. Jewish tradition exhorts males over eighteen to be married. In fact, males over twenty years of age who remained unmarried were said to be cursed by God. That Jesus was not married is conceivably related to Jewish marriage law that prohibited Jews born out of wedlock from marrying an Israelite.[2] Jesus could not identify an earthly father and was considered a bastard. Hence, he was only eligible to marry a Gentile. Further, an intuitive observation suggests the disciples were immature and lacking in savvy. Perhaps their youth was to blame. In fact, they seemed to misunderstand a number of important things Jesus said. Needless to say, a despotic Jesus would never be expected to recruit anyone who would challenge him. In the end, one thing is certain. Jesus was resolute regarding the loyalty he expected. Yet he recruited Judas Iscariot.

Alas, Jesus' initial attempt at interaction with Jewish worshippers was a disaster that almost ended in tragedy. His outspoken and somewhat arrogant demeanor was harshly received. Clearly, he was lacking in people skills. In general, Jesus' early public efforts were only modestly successful. He lost many followers who may have been unimpressed or put off by what he had to say. Jesus' demand for complete surrender may have been viewed as an unreasonable expectation by some. It remains so today.

---

[2] Schechter, Solomon and Greenstone, "Marriage Laws."

His disdain for shared fealty was readily apparent. The underpinning of his appeal to early followers was the allure that came from his messianic claim. People were willing to look past unseemly character faults in order to participate in the Messiah's plan for the future.

However, it is the sincere lack of belief on the part of family and friends that is most revealing. Early in his ministry, Mary and her other children held Jesus out as being mad. Within the framework of his family dynamics, he was acting out of place. Moreover, Jesus' former friends in Galilee, those who watched him grow up, scoffed at his pretense.

How is it, in this modern era, otherwise rational people can be identified who are willing to place faith in a two-thousand-year-old enigmatic actor? Especially after considering that his own family and hometown peers thought he was out of his mind? Let us take a brief look at that before moving deeper into a discussion on the ministry of Jesus.

The Sanity of the Savior

In today's third-millennium society, a person who walks the streets of any municipality, voicing loudly that he is the "Son of God," will doubtlessly be looked upon by passersby as being delusional. Our smart and savvy civilization largely understands mental health issues and consequently indulges those whose plight leaves them out of touch with reality. But even as we sympathize, we may still find them somewhat vexing. Fortunately, compassion overrules, and society extends a hand to help remedy the distress of those who are mentally disadvantaged. From a historical perspective, those beset with mental health problems have not always been treated so kindly. Just a century ago, many with uncontrollable psychoses, behavioral issues, or mood disorders found themselves locked away in insane asylums. Being institutionalized put the unpleasantness of seeing and dealing with so-called crazies out of sight and out of mind.

If Jesus had lived in a different era but behaved as he did in the first century, what would be the prevailing opinion of him? Was Jesus just an attention-seeking impostor whose motives were harmless? If not that, then perhaps a simple charlatan who meant no ill will? Or rather, did his categorically outlandish claims and unconventional behaviors have far-reaching implications that went well beyond such benign descriptions?

It is important to realize that perceptions of mental health issues are relative with respect to contemporaneous time frames. Yesterday's normal behavior may be abnormal today. That is especially true when taking into account how religious influence and cultural norms play a key role in defining the parameters of acceptable behavior. These things must be given consideration when attempting to assess the sanity of the Savior.

Early Observations

In the first century CE, aberrant mental health was largely thought of as being connected to demonic possession. Jesus was accused of being demon-possessed early in his ministry. According to Mark 3:22, scribes from the Temple came forth and made statements regarding their observations of Jesus:

> And the scribes who came down from Jerusalem said, 'He has Beelzebub',

and

> By the ruler of the demons He casts out demons.

Their allegations were harsh in that Beelzebub was one of the seven princes of hell. Christian theology equates Beelzebub with Satan. Hence, Jesus was thought to be possessed by Satan. Of course, Temple authorities may have already developed an unfavorable opinion of Jesus, so perhaps they were giving him a bad rap. His family would know him better than others could. What would they say? "But when His own people [family] heard about this, they went out to lay hold of Him, for they said, 'He is out of His mind'" (Mark 3:21).

It is recorded that early in his ministry, Jesus' family was frantically searching for him as they heard he had been making bizarre comments and casting out demons. Demonstrating their concern for his mental health, his family would feel the need to "lay hold of him" (seize or restrain him) for his own sake. Mark 3:21 describes the episode, which occurred shortly before the scribes accused him of being possessed.

This disquieting event offers insight into what contemporary thinking was regarding the behaviors Jesus demonstrated. Making outlandish claims about himself and intrepidly casting out demons was not considered to be standard behavior, even in the first century. His family agreed with the Temple scribes, which establishes that Jesus was functioning outside of behavioral norms.

It would not be unfair to conjecture that the self-declared savior may have been suffering from a psychiatric condition. Was it mental illness that twisted the mind of Jesus into believing he was God? It does, in fact, seem plausible to think so. Much of what Jesus said would be dismissed as ludicrous by rational persons from any period. His claim to being the Son of God would lead to ridicule in most cultures, past and present. Paradoxically, however, leaders of many ancient civilizations professed close connections with deities. It has not always been considered an irrational claim, at least for those who were venerated because of their power and fame. Religious and political figureheads were unashamed in proclaiming their own avatar.

Caesar Augustus considered himself to be the son of a god. His Roman constituency, who believed him, awarded Augustus godhood status upon his death. Egyptian pharaohs were also recognized as gods on earth, as were many others from various cultures and civilizations. So then, what was it that distinguished Jesus from other self-professed deities? One guess is that his lowly class status and provincial station likely had much to do with it. He had no standing in his own country and was a nobody. Hence, he lacked essential god-validating prerequisites and was considered by his contemporaries to be just another peasant claiming to be God.

To thoroughly investigate whether Jesus was of sound mind would require pertinent sources of information. Outside of the scriptures, there is a paucity of documentation that relates to him. Unfortunately, there is not much to go on. It remains to be seen what kind of mental health diagnoses, if any, Jesus would incur if evaluated today. A few possibilities might be worth taking a look at.

Schizophrenia

It is no secret that, across time, Jesus has been considered delusional by many observers. Delusions of grandeur are a predominant symptom that presents in schizophrenia. The delusions are frequently represented by an individual's belief that he is someone other than who he is. The assumed identity is usually a supernatural figure or celebrity. Along those lines, Jesus thought he was the Son of God, the Hebrew Messiah, and the Savior.

Schizophrenics may also believe they have special abilities and powers. Miraculous healing skills and the ability to raise the dead would qualify. As was also the case with Jesus, schizophrenic delusions are primarily focused on God, or themes that center on good versus evil. Further, because they suffer from paranoia, schizophrenics are prone to imagine they are victims of various conspiratorial plots. They may be fearful that someone, or something, is out to get them. Because of that, they are preoccupied with concerns that relate to loyalty. Jesus insisted on unfettered fealty.

Hallucinations, both auditory and visual, are another symptom that sometimes plagues schizophrenics. It is common for schizophrenics to hear voices and see things that are not there.[1] Jesus claimed to hear the physical voice of God on more than one occasion (e.g., 2 Pet. 1:17–19 and Matt. 3:17).

Episodic rage is a characteristic of schizophrenia that may have played an important role in Jesus' demise. Personal stressors, like the circumstances Jesus faced during his last Passover week, commonly predispose schizophrenics to uncontrolled violent outbursts. It would be germane if we could determine that the violence against the Temple money changers was spawned by schizophrenia.

Symptoms of schizophrenia can wax and wane. Schizophrenics may go through periods where they seem quite normal. With medication, symptoms can be controlled somewhat. Without medication, a small percentage of schizophrenics may achieve a limited capacity to manage their symptoms.

Jesus' claims to raising the dead, healing the sick, and making the blind see are fantastical by contemporary standards. As mentioned, they are consistent with schizophrenic-based grandiose thinking. Today, those kinds of alleged healings are limited to the work of shamans and witch doctors—healers who are part of mostly traditional cultures. They are often hidden in the shadows and away from critical observation. Jesus was not so different. He performed the majority of his alleged healings in far-flung and sparsely populated territories in and around Galilee.

---

[1] "Hallucinations, Optimism Help Maintain Grandiose Delusions."

The Mind of Jesus—What Others Thought

Numerous investigators have pursued the question of Jesus' sanity. The first to do so in the modern era was French psychologist Charles Binet-Sanglé. He published his opinions on Jesus in his 1918 book *La Folie de Jesus* (On the Madness of Jesus). Binet-Sanglé felt strongly that Jesus was afflicted with religious paranoia.[2] That diagnosis no longer exists as such, but has instead been absorbed by other recognized psychiatric disorders.

Professor Justin Meggitt of the University of Cambridge contributed in his book, *The Madness of King Jesus: Why was Jesus Put to Death, but his Followers were not?*, that Pilate and other Roman authorities regarded Jesus as being an "insane and deceptive lunatic".[3] There was a reluctance to crucify a man whose chief offense was being mentally unstable. Pilate's mockery and scorn revealed that he had no fear of Jesus. It is ironic, however, that in taking Jesus seriously, the Chief Priests, elders, and scribes bestowed him with credibility. It yielded the impression that he was someone to be feared. His violent outburst at the Temple courtyard notwithstanding, had they treated him as just another harmless messianic claimant, his blasphemous words may have fallen on deaf ears. Putting him in jail might have demonstrated to his rapidly dwindling base that he was powerless to rescue himself. Once Passover week had concluded, and local life returned to normal, they could have released him to endure public ridicule. Perhaps the Temple authorities decided that in moving to crucify Jesus, he would be forced to save himself. Failure to do so would signify that he was not the Messiah. Following his death, there was no riot or uprising of any kind.

Narcissism

It is possible that Jesus suffered from some other type of mental health diagnosis. Some suggest bipolar disorder. Others lean toward

---

[2] Sanglé-Binet," *La folie de Jesus*.
[3] Meggitt, *The Madness of King Jesus*.

a mood or personality disorder. One that does pique interest is narcissism.

According to the *Diagnostic and Statistical Manual of Mental Disorders* (DSM-5), the essential feature of Narcissistic Personality Disorder is a pervasive pattern of grandiosity, need for admiration, and a lack of empathy. Jesus clearly had little or no empathy toward his family. He was often rude to his mother. By the same token, his miracles were often self-serving and did not always come from a place of mercy. Some of his alleged miracles were done merely to satisfy prophecies. He performed messianic miracles to prove he was the Messiah. There are even reports that he did healings reluctantly, and then, only for Jews. (Jesus did not care for Gentiles until he found he needed their numbers to prevent his cause from failing).

In his book *God Has a Narcissistic Personality Disorder*, Andrew Jasko points out that narcissists "aggressively devalue or destroy those who threaten their self-image." He then goes on to explain, "Narcissists may appear charming and benevolent at first, but they merely feign empathy in order to exploit people whom they use as objects to get what they want".[4]

Jesus was seen by many as arrogant, self-centered, and demanding. He seemed to need excessive praise and admiration. He claimed to be God incarnate and declared he was "the way, truth and the life" (John 14:6). While he demanded that people around him be of service, he falsely claimed that it was he who was a servant. When things failed to go his way, Jesus could get irate. All of these traits are common to narcissism.

Very similar to narcissism is the mental state known as megalomania. Megalomaniacs are obsessed with power and feelings of grandiosity. They have delusional fantasies regarding their own importance. Megalomaniacs can be dictatorial as they value their personal opinions above all others and believe those opinions are infallible. They often engage in belittling others as a byproduct of their inflated self-esteem. It would *not* be unfair to speculate that Jesus of Nazareth possessed traits that were common to narcissistic personality disorder or megalomania.

---

[4] Jasko, "God Has a Narcissistic Personality Disorder."

Demon Possession

The topic of demonic possession is included here as collateral information, given that Jesus was involved in exorcising demons as a way to treat many illnesses. By the same token, he had himself been accused of being demon possessed.

Demonic possession, also called spirit possession, depending on the culture, is a circumstance where a spirit or demon enters a human body and seeks to control, oppress, and torment the victim (host). There is no direct evidence that demons can inflict physical injury or disease on humans. Conceivably, mental stress can suppress immune responses thus allowing opportunistic pathogens to flourish. Commonly, those who appear to be possessed may fail to eat and can consequently become thin or anorexic. Physical contortion and self-harming may leave victims injured. Without supporting evidence, a number of evangelical and charismatic churches posit unapologetically that demon possession is responsible for chronic fatigue syndrome, homosexuality, alcoholism, and addiction to pornography.[5]

Characteristics associated with demon possession are numerous. The lengthy list includes demonstrations of superhuman strength, possession of knowledge the victim could not know, the ability to speak in unknown languages, obscene hand gestures, and vile cursing. Rage, taunting, extreme contortions, and the ability to speak with diverse phonations are additional presenting behaviors. The most extreme manifestations include levitation and the ability to move objects using telekinesis.

There is only one direct mention of demonic possession in the Old Testament. The apparent case involved King Saul. 1 Samuel 16:14 speaks of Saul being "tormented" by an evil spirit. There is no mention of Saul actually being possessed. Rather, the verse states he was tormented. There is one other possible mention of demon possession described in the 22nd chapter of 1 Kings. It relates how false prophets used by King Ahab were said to be empowered by "a deceiving spirit." Accounts of demon possession in the New Testament include, but are not limited to, the demons known

---

[5] Tennant, "In Need of Deliverance."

collectively as "legion," who were cast out from the maniac of Gaderenes, and the seven demons Jesus cast out of Mary Magdalene. Given the paucity of possession references in the Old Testament, it is somewhat surprising to find that demons and demonic possession are extremely common in the New Testament. At least twenty-five passages describe Jesus casting out demons.

In an article written for the *Washington Post*, Dr. Richard Gallagher, board-certified psychiatrist, divulges unique aspects of his work with church-affiliated exorcists. Originally a skeptic who was trained in physical science, mental health, and medicine, Dr. Gallagher now says, "I believe I've seen the real thing." Activity he claims to have witnessed includes verbal expressions of hidden knowledge, the ability to speak unknown foreign languages, and uncommon feats of strength. He has not seen levitation, but he has worked with people who vowed they have. Dr. Gallagher reports that the overwhelming majority of alleged possessions are explained by mental illness. However, there are enough seemingly authentic possessions that the Catholic Church maintains fifty trained and certified exorcists who handle roughly twenty inquiries per week in the U.S.[6]

An article published in the *Journal for the Scientific Study of Religion* reported that "possession case histories consistently reflect a tendency toward hysterical features, sometimes in conjunction with neurotic depression." Further, the report stated that "possession affords two positive advantages to the individual—direct escape from a conflict situation and diminution of guilt by projecting blame onto the intruding spirit".[7] This study implicates mental health problems as the scientific basis for alleged demonic possession. It also widens causation to encompass certain psychological benefits, such as escapism and the redirection of guilt. Even though studies of this nature point to mental health issues as being primarily responsible for alleged possessions, there have been a few other studies reporting that epilepsy is still being confused with demon possession in some cultures. Less frequently, there are instances noted where seizure activity co-presents with hysteria.

---

[6] Gallagher, "As a Psychiatrist."
[7] Ward and Beaubrun, "The Psychodynamics of Demon Possession."

It seems incongruous that Jesus attributed many pathological conditions, both physical and mental, to demon possession. It is counterintuitive that a man who called himself God did not even know the nature of what it was he was healing. *His level of understanding was not consistent with the role he claimed.*

***

Commentary

Jesus of Nazareth was an extraordinary individual. He did not fit any pre-existing mold. Even now, he seems to defy comprehension. As such, Jesus remains an enigmatic historical figure to this day. Perhaps all we can safely say is that he was "not normal." The question goes begging, however: Does *not normal* correspond to *mentally ill* when it comes to the self-proclaimed Son of God?

There is no doubt that Jesus was observed to be mentally ill early in his ministry. It is significant that among those making the accusations were his own family members, not to mention prominent individuals from the Temple. Other early followers walked away, put off by his message. Jesus continued with his ministry in spite of the early losses and allegations of demonic possession.

Some of his successes must have been attributable, in part, to his intellectual prowess. He was smart when it came to implementing and navigating his plan. But where was he going with it? In claiming to be the Messiah, he was clearly eager to assume that role. He persisted in seeking messianic recognition until the end. What if the Hebrew hierarchy had said "Yes"? How then would Jesus have satisfied his professed role as sacrificial Savior? Would he have called upon an angelic army to remove the occupying Romans? Indeed, if Jesus had gotten his way after all, a multitude of serious theological and logistical questions arise. Did he really think it through?

Undeniably, when it was time for Jesus to make good on his promises, he fell far short. More than likely, he had been bluffing all along. If Jesus was perfectly sane and mentally healthy, his life would have played out in a way that was consistent with stability.

Individuals who are mentally stable do not wake up one morning and decide to don the mantle of God. Was Jesus who he said he was? If one chooses to believe such a thing, then rational explanations are being overlooked. For most of us, the evidence is stacking up against the playacting Son of God.

The Ministry of Jesus

Some 13.8 billion years following the birth of the known universe, Jesus of Nazareth began his ministry. It would last between one to three years and would cover a small area of the Middle East region that is presently home to the nation-state of Israel. Reports on the ministry of Jesus that are contemporary to his time do not exist. Rather, the record of his accomplishments is laid out in the New Testament, which was generated to tell his story. The ministry of Jesus produced nothing of factual significance, and much of what was written regarding it was the elaborate creation of many of his early followers. Those who created and then embellished the works of Jesus did so because they stood to gain financially from seeing church membership increase. The early church then became wealthy as new believers were coerced into giving all they had. An example of this is chronicled in Acts 4:34–5:11:

> Nor was there anyone among them who lacked; for all who were possessors of land or houses sold them, and brought the proceeds of the things that were sold, and laid them at the apostle's feet. And Joses...a Levite of the country of Cyprus, having land, sold it, and brought the money and laid it at the apostle's feet. But a certain man named Ananias, with Sapphira his wife, sold a possession; And he kept back part of the proceeds...and brought a certain part and laid it at the apostle's feet.

In spite of the prudent donation that Ananias and Saphirra had given, they nevertheless came under criticism from Peter, who angrily accused them of holding back on God. The apostle made the accusation that in failing to give *all* of the proceeds to the church, they had been guilty of lying to the Holy Spirit. Out of abject fear, both Ananias and his wife fell to the ground, dead. This event was used to strike terror into the hearts of the early church membership. As recorded in Acts 5:11, "Great fear came upon the church and upon all who heard these things."

The willingness of the apostles to employ fear and intimidation in exploiting new followers must be considered when assessing their motivations for growing the church. Conceivably, it was wealth that provided the primary incentive for inserting embellished accounts of Jesus into the New Testament. Likewise, it may well have been money that was behind their zeal for the cause of Christ. After all, there was little to be made by fishing. They now had a celebrity and a cause that could foster a new and more lucrative way of life. This postulate is not far-fetched. History records that most human activity has been motivated by making money. Keeping this in mind, the ministry of Jesus, as recorded in the New Testament, must be examined from a keenly skeptical perspective.

Miracles

The ministry of Jesus began in the district around Galilee. It involved preaching, teaching, and, allegedly, healing. It was during that period that Jesus was said to perform many miracles. It was claimed that he healed the sick, made the blind see, and even raised a few from the dead. Other miracles included walking on water (Matt. 14:22–33) and feeding a crowd of 5,000 with just five loaves of bread and two small fish (Matt. 14:31, Luke 9:12–17). Altogether there are thirty-seven miracles recorded in the New Testament. Only three miracles are reported in all four Gospels, however. Of these three, the most significant is considered to be Jesus' own resurrection, for which there is no true evidence. Jesus performed miracles to give credibility to his claim of being God. They were considered signs and wonders that only someone with supernatural powers could perform. We cannot know with certainty that any of this truly happened. It takes a willingness to accept that notion. Of course, that is the driving power behind blind faith.

Numerous miracles are recorded in both the Old and New Testaments. Moses was alleged to have performed a number of miracles. They included the Egyptian plagues, the parting of the Red Sea, and the striking of a rock to produce water. His brother Aaron had a magic staff that turned into a serpent and later bloomed after sprouting in the desert. Joshua miraculously brought down the impregnable wall of Jericho. There were many more that God performed through those who were considered righteous and faithful.

Miracles of the New Testament center on Jesus, but he is not alone in performing them. Matthew 10:1 and 10:8 describe how Jesus sent his disciples out to teach, preach, and heal. It is said he conveyed to them the power to heal the sick, cleanse lepers, raise the dead, and cast out demons. Peter healed a crippled beggar and a bedridden paralytic, raised Dorcas-Tabitha from the dead, and healed "crowds of sick and those tormented by evil spirits" (Acts 5:14–15). Remarkably, Christians credit Peter with a miracle for using his divine power, bestowed by Jesus, to kill Ananias and Sapphira (above). Most would consider that a form of murder, but there are believers who think otherwise. The Apostle Paul performed a sizeable number of miracles, most of which are reported in the book of Acts, which he co-authored. (View with suspicion those purported miracles that are recorded by the one who supposedly performed them.) Christians typically believe that miracles happening outside the context of faith are either misreported or are hoaxes. However, some evangelical believers feel miraculous events can occur outside of an explicitly Christian setting, if it serves God's purpose.

That Jesus of Nazareth was considered a deity because he claimed to perform miracles falls short in terms of being a qualifying determinant. There have been a multitude of religious practitioners who proclaimed their ability to perform miraculous stunts of all kinds. Mohammed and Buddha are just two examples. Then consider that every saint venerated by the Catholic Church must have performed at least two miracles. Clearly, miracles alone do not convey godhood or deity to anyone. And of course, that assumes said miracles are not trickery, illusion, coincidence, or fake news.

Healing miracles that appear authentic presumably stem from the human mind and the power of suggestion. The placebo effect, the power of belief, hypnosis, and the recently discovered "internal pharmacy" can all produce astonishing results that may appear miraculous in origin.[1]

The suspect idea that the Hebrew Messiah would perform miracles arises primarily from the New Testament. Old Testament references to healing miracles include Isaiah 29:18 and Isaiah 35:5. The context of Isaiah 29:18 concerns situations that are only allegorically related to healing. The metaphorical phrases "the deaf shall hear" and "the eyes of the blind shall be opened" speak to the return of the people from the blindness that moral decay and disobedience to God brought with it. It represents a restoration of wisdom and not a miraculous physical healing. Isaiah 35:5–6 speaks to the joy of those whom God heals spiritually. The idea that these verses are messianic prophecies regarding miraculous physical healing by Jesus of Nazareth is contrived.

Christians sometimes reference four "messianic miracles." They are.

1. The cleansing of a leper
2. The casting out of a *deaf and dumb* demon
3. The healing of birth defects
4. The raising of the dead after three days

The casting out of a deaf and dumb demon implies that being deaf and mute is not related to physical pathologies, but rather, is the result of an evil spirit. Mark 9:27–28 reports on the failure of the disciples to cast out a demon from a deaf and mute child who, in reality, appeared to be having a grand mal seizure. Jesus effectively told them that some kinds of demons "can go out by nothing, but prayer and fasting." He was essentially saying to give it some time and it will pass. That is particularly true when epileptic seizures are involved.

Grand mal, or tonic-clonic, seizures represent a type of epileptic seizure that begins with a short duration loss of consciousness. Violent seizure activity that includes hyper-rigidity of muscles and the clenching of teeth follows. There is frequently a shout (ictal cry) that results from a strong contraction of the larynx

---

[1] Vance, "The Science Behind Miracles."

and expiratory muscles. Finally, there is a characteristic relaxation of the musculature that is most often accompanied by a lack of responsiveness. These symptoms are *identical* to the symptoms that occurred in the "miracle" described in Mark 9:27–28.

While conversing with the boy's father and others, Jesus appeared to be waiting for the seizure to run its course. He commanded the demon to come out near the end of the episode. Jesus then picked the child up off the ground after he regained consciousness. Nowhere does it indicate that the boy's ability to hear and speak had returned. Jesus did not declare it so, but instead, rushed the child into the house and away from the gathered crowd. In this narrative, Jesus feigned an exorcism and received credit for a messianic miracle. To be certain, the so-called miracles of the Bible were not always what they appeared to be.

A somewhat similar situation transpired when Jesus was approached by the Syro-Phoenician woman whose daughter was "severely demon possessed" (Matt. 15:22). Initially Jesus was reluctant to acknowledge the distraught woman, but his disciples pleaded with him to keep her quiet by helping her daughter. Jesus responded by saying, "I was not sent to minister to anyone other than the Jews." Then Jesus spoke directly to the woman, stating, in a reference to Proverbs 9:7–8, "It is not good to take the children's bread and throw it to the little dogs" (Matt. 15:26). Here, the Son of God was not above being rude and condescending when he implied that non-Hebrew children were "little dogs." The woman's clever retort, "Yet even the little dogs eat the crumbs which fall from their master's table," won her what she sought. Exasperated, Jesus liberally interpreted what she had said as showing great faith, "and her daughter was healed from that hour." Jesus never saw the stricken girl, who was homebound. We can surmise that she may have had a seizure disorder and Jesus was hoping the episode would cease by the time the mother returned home. Jesus then quickly departed and headed back to Galilee.

The Miracle at Cana

The earliest reported miracle of Jesus' ministry was the well-known "water-to-wine" event at the wedding in Cana. It is found in John

2:1–12. This reported miracle most likely represents the embellishment of a real event. John may have used the wedding account as a vehicle to portray Jesus' reluctance to move forward with his ministry. In this passage, Jesus clearly seems conflicted.

There have been many exegetical offerings regarding the metaphorical meaning behind the water-to-wine story. Generally, it refers to God's miraculous provision in time of need. Not surprisingly, some Christian commentary seems overly concerned about a literal translation here. To deny that the element of alcohol was involved, fundamental believers must refute the miracle happened.

There is some conjecture that the bride and groom were close to the family of Jesus, and it is implied in the passage regarding the wedding that Mary may have been one of the planners. It was the third day of a week-long wedding feast, and they had already run out of wine. Jesus' mother approached him and said, "They have no wine." Jesus resisted by saying, "Woman, what has that got to do with me? My hour has not yet come."

A complete and accurate understanding of the exchange between Jesus and his mother is lacking. What did Jesus mean by, "My hour has not yet come?" Could his resistance reveal that this was not the way he wanted to publicly unveil who he truly was? He effectively said, "I am not ready for this."

Nevertheless, Jesus acquiesced to his mother's request and had six large jars filled to the brim with water. Each vessel held about thirty gallons, so the amount of wine Jesus provided with this miracle was about 180 gallons. That is a lot of *oinos*! The headmaster of the wedding was thrilled and called the groom over to thank him. "Every man at the beginning sets out the good wine, and when the guests have well drunk, he puts out the inferior wine. You have kept the good wine till now!" There is a clear inference here that the guests had consumed all the wine that was initially provided and that they were "well drunk." For Jesus to provide the inebriated guests with more alcohol contributed to their ongoing intemperance. The New Testament mentions several times that it is a sin to "be drunk with wine." Having contributed to the sin of the wedding celebrants, had Jesus himself sinned? Recognizing the dilemma, many believers say "no." Their assertion is that the wine was not fermented—it was, in actual fact, grape juice. The Greek word *oinos*, as used in the original text, means wine, not grape juice. The vision of party celebrants downing enormous quantities of grape juice is a humorous one.

Modern Magic

There have been those throughout the course of history who performed feats that were considered supernatural or miraculous. Most have not claimed to be God, although some offered that they were inspired by the Holy Spirit. Faith healers are still abundant in today's world. These charlatans put on an emotionally charged show that is often very convincing. Many faith-based healers literally believe they are inspired by God. Some of their followers may be authentically healed for reasons that cannot be well understood. These healings possibly result from the resolution of a psychosomatic illness, or they may simply be born of the placebo effect.[2] The power of suggestion is a mighty tool when used skillfully with desperate and vulnerable people. Most of the hopeful contribute significant amounts of their hard-earned money to these unethical con artists. To some who view this from the outside, it appears to be the stuff of scams and has nothing to do with God except as the blind faith of the believer is involved.

Today there are secular magicians who amaze us with their deception and sleight of hand. Some appear to walk on water or levitate through the air. A few walk convincingly through walls or closed windows. Others disappear or cause observers to do so. Some can read your mind, tell you what is in your pocket, or predict which card you will choose. It all looks quite real and is very compelling. If these entertainers can figure out a ruse, why could Jesus not do the same? In fact, there are those who believe Jesus had learned magic while in Egypt or India, sometime before his ministry began.[3]

There are people who do, indeed, defy logic. Take, for instance, Edgar Cayce. Born in 1877, he was a mystic and clairvoyant who could correctly answer questions about people he

---

[2] "The Placebo Effect: What Is It?"
[3] *The Jewish Encyclopedia*, 171 and Evans, *The Historical Jesus*, 376.

knew nothing about. He could diagnose disease and suggest a remedy just by reading a letter from someone who was suffering. He was accurate at prophecy and foretold things that would later come true. Cayce could lay his head on a book and know everything that was in it, page by page. Much of what he did was authenticated and verified. Yet he never claimed to be God or took advantage of the supernatural abilities he was blessed with. He was, in fact, a devout Christian whose skills eventually brought him into conflict with his beliefs.[4]

The Jesus Seminars

There are scholars who have evaluated the miracles of Jesus and determined that most of them did not actually happen. Of note was the Jesus Seminar, which was active during the 1980s and '90s. This group of about 150 Christian theologians, Bible scholars, and Jesuits gathered to seek out the truth about Jesus. They met twice a year to study the "Sayings of Jesus, the Deeds of Jesus, and the Profiles of Jesus." After each meeting, participants would vote on the questions they had considered. Among their determinations was that only 16% of the miracles attributed to Jesus were authentic. Additionally, they decided that only 18% of the things he was alleged to have said in the Gospels were really his words.[5] Finally, the Seminar examined 387 events found in the Gospels. Those they considered most likely to have occurred were:

1. The Beelzebub controversy (Luke 11:15–17)
2. The voice in the wilderness (Mark 1:18)
3. John's baptism of Jesus (Mark 1:9–11)
4. Jesus proclaiming the "good news" (Mark 1:14–25)
5. The incident with Peter's mother-in-law (Mark 1:29–31)
6. The leper (Matt. 8:1–14)
7. The Paralytic and four (Mark 2:1–12)
8. The call of Levi (Luke 5:27–28)

---

[4] "Edgar Cayce."
[5] Funk, "The Jesus Seminar Phase 2."

9. Dining with sinners (Matt. 9:10–13)
10. Sabbath observance (Mark 2:23–28)

The Fellows of the Seminar concluded that Jesus did not walk on water, feed the multitudes, or raise Lazarus from the dead. The primary reason given for such a low confirmation rate was that little hard evidence supporting the authenticity of the Gospels existed before the end of the second century. Further, there was a consensus that third-generation authors wrote the Gospels late in the first century based on "folk memories preserved in stories that had circulated by word of mouth for decades."[6] Therefore, it is likely that the stories had been shaped and reshaped, embellished and augmented for at least half a century before they were written down.

Preaching and Teaching

The first major discourse delivered by Jesus was the Sermon on the Mount. This eloquent oratory included the well-known Beatitudes as well as the Lord's Prayer. The Bible records it in Matthew, chapters five through seven. Jesus gave four other major sermons, all found in the Gospel of Matthew. The Gospel of John tells of Jesus speaking at four additional gatherings in Jerusalem. John's Gospel is the only one that places him in Jerusalem outside of the week that culminated in his crucifixion. This significant difference between the Gospel of John and the synoptic Gospels raises questions. Was Jesus a Galilean wanderer who stayed away from Jerusalem in order to avoid the Jewish Temple authorities? Or was it his appearances in Jerusalem, as mentioned by John, that eventually started and then promoted the antagonistic relationship Jesus had with those authorities? It seems likely that John writes the more accurate account. It is known that Jesus enjoyed the status of rabbi and that he had taught in the Temple at Jerusalem. Therefore, one would not be amiss in assuming Jesus was in Jerusalem more frequently than the synoptic Gospels indicate.

The fact that Jesus taught in the Temple and elsewhere implies that he spoke fluent Hebrew. He undoubtedly used Hebrew

---

[6] Funk, "Excerpts from the Introduction of the Acts of Jesus."

when teaching and delivering parables. Hebrew was the language traditionally used by rabbis when teaching and performing their official duties. The primary language spoken by Jesus and the apostles was Aramaic. The New Testament also suggests that a few of the apostles might have spoken Greek. Although Philip may have been able to speak Greek, it was his brother Andrew who was approached to translate for Greek-speaking Jews who wanted to meet with Jesus (John 12:20–22). Peter is known to have preached in Greek to Hellenized (Greek-speaking) Jews.

It is curious that Jesus required a translator when he met with Greek-speaking Jews. If he was God, why was it he did not understand every language in existence at a conversant level? It was "the Creator" who gave Adam and Eve the world's first language. It was God who confused language at the Tower of Babel. It was the Holy Spirit who provided translation on the Day of Pentecost. If Jesus, as God, participated in the creation of language, why could he not speak conversant Greek? Why did "God made flesh" need a translator?

The Apostle Paul undoubtedly spoke Greek.[7] Parenthetically, because the early apostles primarily spoke Aramaic, some argue it is unlikely that they would have authored the Gospels, which were written in Greek. This supports the school of thought that credits later authors with being responsible.

Regardless, the ministry of Jesus was headed for a climactic ending. In Luke 9:22–24, Jesus tells the disciples that he would be rejected by the Jewish priests, elders, and scribes, then put to death. Following that, he said he would "be raised again on the third day." Thus, he describes his future crucifixion and resurrection.

***

Commentary

A point that cannot be overlooked regards the fact that Jesus was unequivocal in statements establishing his allegiance to the Jews in terms of ministry. In Matthew 15:24, he made clear that he was sent

---

[7] Brown, "What Language Did Jesus and the Apostles Speak?

from God the father to serve the Jews only. This is in conflict with any notion claiming that Jesus came to "save the *world* from its sins." Matthew 1:21 records the words, "He will save His *people* from their sins" (emphasis mine). This references the Jews who were "His people." The Messiah is a feature of the Hebrew faith. The messianic hope applies only to Jews. Nevertheless, early in his ministry, Jesus sent his disciples out "two by two" (Mark 6:7) to minister and preach in distant outlying areas. Similarly, he sent his followers "into all the world" when issuing his "great commission" (Matt. 28:19). John 3:16–17 clearly reveals that Jesus saw himself as the savior of the entire world —not just the savior of the Jews. Somewhere Jesus had a change of vision. The "when" is hard to ascertain. The "why" most likely relates pragmatically to a lack of Jewish followers.

Magicians have amazed the world with their illusions since the dawn of civilization. Anyone who has witnessed popular illusionist Chris Angel walk atop the waters of a resort pool, or David Blaine as he levitates in front of an awestruck crowd, knows just how far magic has come. Mentalist Derren Brown's TV show "Miracle" makes it clear that healing and deliverance feats are easy to reproduce when a skilled magician is involved. Chris Angel once said that the goal of an illusionist is to "get the audience to believe a lie."

Although the Bible clearly exaggerates and embellishes its accounts, there can be no doubt that real-time deception was likewise an integral part of many miracles. The self-proclaimed Messiah had no qualms about employing deception to fool the masses. That much is obvious from his opportunistic use of epilepsy to feign exorcisms. Deception is dishonesty in action. Dishonesty is a trait that is identified as a moral shortcoming. That fact bodes poorly for the "sinless" Savior.

Expositors typically preach that Jesus taught, healed, and performed miracles during the course of his three-year ministry. They ignore interpretations of the synoptic Gospels that imply the ministry of Jesus lasted only one year. In essence, diminishing his ministry to a single year lessens the perception of its profundity. To consider that Jesus and his message were rapidly dismissed is a stand-alone statement. That is, until it is combined with the fact that his ministry involved itself with Jews only and that it took place over a tiny region of the middle east some 2,000 years ago. Since the Apostle John indirectly relates that it endured for nearly three years, I suppose we could pass it off as just another biblical discrepancy. Unfortunately, sorting out truth from the pages of "God's Word" is proving to be an onerous task.

Creating the Savior Paradigm

In the fifty-third chapter of Isaiah is found the story of the *sin-bearing servant.* (Hebrew, *suffering* servant.) Without knowing the truthful Hebrew application of this passage, it superficially appears that it is allegorical in a way that fits the person of Jesus, especially in light of how his life played out. The sin-bearing servant was prophesied to be "despised and rejected by men" (Isa. 53:3). That was indeed the fate of the Christian Christ. The verses found in Isaiah 53 tell the story of how Jesus may have foreseen his future fate:

> But He was wounded for our transgressions, He was bruised for our iniquities; The punishment for our peace was upon Him. And by His stripes we are healed (Isa. 53:5).

> All we like sheep have gone astray; We have turned, every one, to his own way. And the Lord has laid on Him the iniquity of us all (Isa. 53:6).

> He was oppressed and afflicted, yet He opened not His mouth. He was led like a lamb to the slaughter (Isa. 53:7).

In the first century, it was the common practice of Jewish landlords to select a single slave (servant) to bear the punishment for all his slaves. This occurred when they failed to accomplish what the master had expected of them. Not wanting to kill or injure them all, the lord would select the most unliked and unproductive individual to bear the punishment for the entire group. The example set by the transference of punishment to one individual was meant to deter future transgressions. The fifty-third chapter of Isaiah is directly related to this practice.

The Judeo-Christian Old Testament uses the term *sin-bearing servant*, while the Hebrew Bible uses the term *suffering servant*. The difference is significant since the term "sin-bearing" equates to the atoning nature of Jesus' death as advocated by Christianity. The connotation of "suffering servant," according to Hebrew theology, metaphorically refers to the Jewish nation and the suffering it was subjected to under Assyria, Babylonia, Greece, and Rome. According to Rabbi Marshall Roth, "In order to properly understand these verses, one must read the original Hebrew text."[1] Rabbi Roth is highly critical of Christian translations of the Hebrew Bible, which "are not rooted in Jewish sources and often go against traditional Jewish teachings."[1] Further, he accuses modern Christian translations as being "even more divorced from the true meaning of the text."[1] This is another example of how the Christian Old Testament revises the true meanings of the Hebrew Bible to suit Christian theology.

The Impossible Role: Savior and Messiah

Jesus saw himself as *the Savior*. It is not established how he reconciled being the Savior with also being the Messiah. Such a thing would be impossible under the tenets of Judaism. Christianity is unwavering in claiming Jesus was both a sacrificial savior and the Jewish Messiah. Hebraic doctrine emphatically rejects that claim.

According to Rabbi Moshe Shulman, "Judaism *never* believed in a Messiah who would come into this world to suffer and die as the Christians did." He further states, "Christians today assume it was all part of the original plan of God as mapped out in the Old Testament. But in fact, the idea of a suffering Messiah cannot be found there. It had to be created."[2] In his book *A Jewish Understanding of the World,* John Rayner writes, "The whole complex of doctrines about the Son of God who died on the Cross to save humanity from sin and death—is incompatible with Judaism."[3]

---

[1] Roth, "Isaiah 53: The Suffering Servant."
[2] Shulman, "Judaism and a Dying Messiah."
[3] Rayner, *A Jewish Understanding of the World*, 187.

There is no dispute that the Messiah was prophesied to be a direct descendant of King David. David, being human, was born into the original sin of Adam. *Therefore, the Messiah, who will descend from the seed of David, was never intended to be a blameless sacrificial savior, as he would of necessity been born into and blemished by original sin.*

In Psalm 51:5, David states, "Behold, I was brought forth in iniquity, and in sin my mother conceived me."

Christian theology has attempted to intercept this crucial problem by naming the Holy Spirit as the father of Jesus. This was done, in part, to eliminate the difficulty created by original sin as it pertains to the Messiah. However, taking this approach has forced Christian theology to find another way to satisfy the requirement of Davidic lineage—a way that places Jesus in the House of David even though he was not born into it. Unfortunately, as we have already discussed, there is no legitimate way to accomplish such a thing. *For Jews, the roles of Messiah and sinless sacrificial savior are incompatible.* Therefore, the claim by Jesus that he was both is spurious. Further, Judaism considers that the Messiah will save the Jewish people from their oppressors and not their sins. These polemics undercut the contention that Jesus was who he said he was. He was properly rejected as the Messiah, due in part to a core theological conflict.

New Testament Christianity borrows from the substitutional atonement story of Abraham and his son Isaac, then merges it with the sin-bearing servant of Isaiah 53. The resulting sacrificial lamb who dies on behalf of all humanity is the person of Jesus Christ. However, since "Christ" means Messiah, it is only appropriate to call him Jesus. He does not fit the mold for the Jewish Messiah and has yet to accomplish anything that the Messiah was supposed to do.

The traditional Jewish concept of the Messiah (*Mashiach* in Hebrew) is one of a king who will restore the glory of the Davidic Dynasty. The term messiah literally means "the anointed one." It refers to the ancient practice of anointing kings with oil when they took the throne. The term *mashiach* does not in any way mean savior. It is derived from the root word *Mem-Shin-Chet*, which means to paint, smear, or anoint. The Christian concept of the Messiah is a distorted one that is based on the word *moshiah*, the

Hebrew root of which is *Yod-Shin-Ayin*. (*Moshiah* is not the same word as *Moshiach*, which is an alternative spelling of *Mashiach*.) *Yod-Shin-Ayin* means "to help or save."[4] It is, in part, this fraudulent meaning used by Christianity that is responsible for much of the confusion as to who Jesus actually was. Christianity has created a semantic ruse in order to make Jesus the Christ.

According to the Talmud, as well as the Mishnah, the Messiah is prophesied to be a human being who is the child of two human parents. The Messiah is foreordained to reinstate the royal Dynasty of David. He will build the Third Temple and restore sacrificial worship. Further, he will live and reign for a very long time. After his death, his son will then reign as king. After his son's death, it is his grandson who will reign over the Jews. Following the reign of the Messiah's grandson, the world will end through apocalypse. It will then "lie dormant" for one thousand years, after which there will be a new Heaven and a new Earth. The Messiah will then rule over Heaven and Earth for ever and ever.[5]

Supersessionism

Even more unprincipled is the belief, held and taught by Christian theology, that Judaism has been supplanted by Christianity. Labeled *replacement theology*, this doctrinal stance, also known as *supersessionism*, teaches that the covenant between God and his chosen people, Israel, was broken. It audaciously asserts that Jesus' "New Covenant" takes precedence over most of the Mosaic Covenant and abrogates the Davidic Covenant. Supersessionism also opens Christianity to the non-Jews of the world. At the same time, it makes Christians God's chosen people while it throws the spiritually orphaned Jews into the streets. That is, unless they bow down before Jesus and accept him as their savior.

In Psalm 2:7 David wrote, "I will declare the decree: The Lord has said to me, You are My son. Today I have begotten you." Hebraic theology has long taught that this verse, and the entire second psalm, is a messianic prophecy. However, it is not messianic

---

[4] Rich, "Maschiah."
[5] "What the Messiah is Supposed to Do."

regarding Jesus of Nazareth as erroneously stated in Acts 13:23 and twice in the book of Hebrews. Rather, it is messianic regarding the future hope of the seed of David.

Psalm 89:27–29 recites the terms of God's covenant with David: "Also, I will make My firstborn, the highest of the kings of the earth. My mercy will I keep for him forever, And *My covenant will stand firm with him. His seed also I will make to endure forever.*" Yahweh also declared: "My covenant I will not break, nor alter the thing that has gone out of my lips...I will not lie unto David" (Ps. 89:34). This promise underscores that the Davidic Covenant will not be broken or added to. Nor will it be used as a springboard to yet another covenant.

Psalm 89 proceeds to describe how the sons of David will continue to rule after him. It is this model that establishes God's plan for the Messiah. In Jeremiah 31:31, God once again refers to this covenant with David as "a new covenant—*one that will never end*". One where God promises to *"forgive their iniquity" and* "remember their sin no more." Jesus would step over this covenant and offer a proxy version that would substitute himself for David and David's descendants. He would make his own "new covenant" and claim that it was he who would deliver the Jews from their sins. Not surprisingly, Jesus took from Psalm 2:7 and proclaimed it was *he* who was the only begotten Son of God. Obviously, this presents a dilemma. There cannot be two "begotten Sons of God" if one of them is claiming to be the "only" begotten Son of God.

Psalm 2:7 represents one of many passages in the Old Testament that Christianity has taken out of context and applied to Jesus. Christians maintain that this verse, and many others in the Hebrew Bible, are prophetic regarding their Christ. The founding scribes of Christianity, writing on behalf of the early apostolic church, nuanced and distorted sacred textual meanings found in the Tanakh. The Gospel authors and the Apostle Paul were primary among them. It is as if these Jewish apostates had forgotten, or perhaps dismissed, that God inspired the words of sacred Jewish texts in a way that was understood and taught by Jewish priests and rabbis for hundreds of years. The covenants God made with Moses and Abraham assured the fathers of Judaism that he would be with his chosen people, and that he would guide and direct them forever

(Jer. 31:3). This meant that God would reveal his truths to the Jewish people and their religious leaders in an inspired way that was not open to doubt or uncertainty. *God's words are supposed to be immutable. His sacred words to his chosen people should be above reinvention by Christianity.*

False Prophet and False Messiah

Jews of today continue their long wait for the Messiah. They are not deterred by the arrogance of Christianity. They believe that at some point the Messiah will appear and restore the royal Davidic Dynasty. His mission will be signified by the building of the Third Temple and in restoring traditional Jewish worship there. In the time of Jesus, when the seventy-week prophecy of Daniel was due to be fulfilled, the Second Temple was already in place on the Temple Mount. In and of itself, that fact casts a shadow of doubt on Daniel's prophecy. Why would the Messiah need to build the Temple when the Temple was already built?

Maimonides, a renowned Jewish philosopher who lived in the twelfth century, firmly believed that Daniel was a false prophet and that his seventy-week prophecy was also false. In fact, many of Daniel's prophecies did fail to materialize. In addition to affecting Daniel's credibility, this also contributes to the assertion that scripture is not inerrant. Further, if the prophecy of Daniel 9 is false, Christianity has little left to hang its hat on. This prophecy plays a key role in establishing for Christians that Jesus was the Messiah.

Perhaps of greater significance is that Maimonides also declared Jesus to be a false messiah. He felt that any messiah who was put to death could not be the true Messiah. It stands to reason that Yahweh would never permit his son—his chosen one—to be killed. Such a thing would represent biblical perversion since God's authority, established in the Hebrew Bible, would need to be subordinated to and overruled by the will of man.

Today's Christians believe in two different resolutions to the problems of the Temple, Daniel's prophecy, and the time of Jesus. Obviously, both solutions cannot be correct. Several Christian denominations are of the opinion that the seventy-week prophecy of Daniel was fulfilled by Jesus when his death on the cross did away with the need for sacrifices. However, it is not clear how this opinion results in the satisfaction of the traditional, or essential, messianic obligations. More importantly, it ignores the need for the Messiah to reinstate sacrificial worship in the rebuilt Temple. That prophecy must be fulfilled. If Jesus was the final sacrifice, part of the prophecy would be negated or even declared false.

The second opinion of mainstream Christianity is that the prophecy of Daniel has not yet been fulfilled. This group proposes a "gap" between weeks sixty-nine and seventy of the prophecy. The completion of the seventieth week will occur, they believe, at the end of the Great Tribulation (apocalypse). It will be signified by the second coming of Jesus and the installation of his kingdom on Earth.[6] The last seven days of the prophecy are represented by the seven years of tribulation. Christians believe it is during this time of tribulation that the Third Temple will be built.

The gap scenario is designed to explain why Jesus did not fulfill the messianic role. It allows for him to do so somewhere down the road. That road is now 2,000 years long. Jewish scholars say there is nothing in scripture that speaks to a "gap" in Daniel's prophecy. They contend it was created by Christians who had to somehow rationalize the problem of Jesus dying.

In all honesty, this is a confusing and convoluted prophecy that has generated several exegetical offerings. It has also helped spawn the fallacious doctrine of supersessionism. One thing that it does for certain is point to the divergence of scriptural interpretation that is held by those who draw their inspiration from the Bible. Further, it demonstrates how one religious group can steal from a more established religion in order to create their own versions of central doctrine.

Who Am I?

How Jesus intended to establish, and then dispatch, his role as the Jewish Messiah no doubt remained unclear to his followers. Indeed, even the disciples seemed curiously unsure of who he was. In Mark 8:27 Jesus asked them, "Who do men say that I am?" In verse 28

---

[6] Ice, "Why a Gap in Daniel's 70 Weeks?"

they answered: "John the Baptist; some say Elijah; and others say one of the prophets." Then Jesus asked them, "But who do you say that I am?" Peter spoke up and answered, "You are the Christ." Jesus' reply was unexpected. He affirmed he was the Christ, yet warned the disciples that they should tell no one about him. But why?

To try and answer that question we must revisit the discourse of Luke 9:22–24. "And Jesus began to teach them that the Son of Man, must suffer many things, and be rejected by the elders and chief priests and scribes, and be killed and after three days, rise again." This was the first time Jesus revealed the crucifixion-resurrection storyline to the disciples. (Many scholars feel this passage, as well as Luke 9:44, was added after the fact.) It might also offer insight as to where he was now placing the emphasis regarding the role he envisioned he would soon occupy. It is inferred that, by telling the disciples not to call him the Christ, he was preparing to cast off that persona. Yet he would continue to plead his case to the chief priests and Pharisees, in the hope they would relent and support his appointment as Messiah. The alternative meant rejection, and his newly revealed role as a martyr. In fact, the rejection that Jesus predicted was not far off.

The Rejected Argument and the Rejected Messiah

In his last confrontational conversation with the Pharisees, Jesus again argued fruitlessly, and for the final time, that he was the Messiah. This discourse is found in Matthew 22: "While the Pharisees were gathered together, Jesus asked them, saying, 'What do you think about the Christ? Whose son is He?' They said to Him, 'The Son of David.' He said to them, 'How then does David in the Spirit call Him 'Lord'? 'If David calls Him "Lord" how is He his son?'" (Matt. 22:41–45).

The Pharisees, appearing to lack a clear understanding of what Jesus said, walked away. Their answer, "The Son of David," was correct in the context of who they knew the Messiah was going to be. Jesus was attempting to convince them by presenting a hypothetical wherein a father (David) is compelled to call his messianic son *Lord*. Although a weak argument, Jesus felt it was important and insisted that such a circumstance cannot be. In attempting a resolution, Jesus rhetorically proposes that *he* can be the Messiah as he is *not* David's son—he is God's son. It was this hand that Jesus played in attempting to establish and justify his authority. Under the guise of being the Son of God, he believed *he* had the self-endowed right to change the prophetic and sacred seed of David decree. Unfortunately for Jesus, the Pharisees did not feel his arguments were cogent. Nor, after knowing him for years, did they believe he was the Son of God. Further, they did not feel he possessed the authority to unilaterally change the Yahweh-given requisites for wearing the crown of *Mashiach ben David*.

And so, the Jewish religious establishment rejected Jesus' claim to being the Christ. In truth, a chance never existed that the Jewish hierarchy would accept him as the Messiah. There were many legitimate reasons that could be used against him. For one, they did not believe that his intentions were consistent with the Messiah's mission. Nor did they accept that he had demonstrated the capability to remove the Romans from Jerusalem. They also saw Jesus as a sinner, for he had healed and performed work on the Sabbath. And, finally, they believed Jesus was a pretender to the throne as he did not possess the bloodline that would allow him to claim his place in the House of David. This wholesale rejection angered Jesus to the point that most of the chapter following this encounter, Matthew 23, is an irate excoriation of those same religious authorities. With loud shouts of anger, he labeled them "hypocrites" and "fools." Soon the animosity became so intense that the Jewish authorities felt compelled to follow through with their plot to kill him.

The Mount of Olives

Following his woeful meeting with the Pharisees, chief priests, and scribes, Jesus went out to the Mount of Olives and talked to his disciples about the end of the age and his second coming. He put forth visions of the terror that would accompany the tribulation (apocalypse), and he explained the signs they should look for portending its beginning. However, of the many things he told his

Creating the Savior Paradigm 65

disciples that day, perhaps nothing was as significant as the so-called fig tree prophecy. If it is interpreted correctly, this prophecy establishes a theoretical window for when Jesus will return. If he does not return by this date, it might well be said that he never will.

The fig tree in the Old Testament has traditionally been regarded as a symbol for Israel. Some, however, have said it is more consistent with the city of Jerusalem. One way or the other, either interpretation plays into the prophecy. The fig tree prophecy was spoken as a parable to the disciples of Jesus. It is part of a long monologue that was in answer to questions put forth in Matthew 24:3: "Now as He sat on the Mount of Olives, the disciples came to Him privately, saying, 'Tell us when these things will be? And what will be the sign of Your coming, and of the end of the age?'" Although Jesus answered with many signs (wars, earthquakes, famine, lawlessness), his final answer came down to the parable of the fig tree. Here is his exposition of it to the inquisitive disciples:

> Now learn this parable from the fig tree: When its branch has already become tender and puts forth leaves, you know that summer is near. So you also, when you see all these things, know that it is near—at the door! Assuredly, I say unto you, this generation will by no means pass away till all these things come to pass (Matt. 24:32–35 [NKJ]).

What exactly does this metaphorical message signify? First of all, there is a significant dispute as to what it means. That is because, as mentioned, one interpretation fixes a date for when Jesus will return. Bible eschatologists are hesitant to go out on that limb. Because of that, they refute the most compelling interpretation. It is as follows:

The fig tree is the last tree in spring to put forth its leaves. It was a propitious and monumental day in history when Israel became a nation-state on May 14, 1948. For almost 2,000 years the Jewish people were scattered around the world. They were often persecuted and reviled. Bible scholars, in general, do not tend to dispute that the rebirth of Israel represents the event where the fig tree put forth its leaves. If they do disagree, it is maintained that the budding fig tree is simply a metaphor for the point where all these things come to pass and the second coming of Christ is then imminent. According to them, the prophecy has nothing to do with the State of Israel. There is nothing unusual about wars, earthquakes, famine, and those other things that Jesus foretold would mark the end of days. Such calamities have always plagued humankind. The only event that is truly remarkable in the prophecy is the founding of modern Israel as represented by the budding fig tree. Those who downplay the importance of the budding fig tree seem to also ignore the sentence that incorporates a generational component to the prophecy. In effect, the skeptics have completely dismantled it.

Those who read the prophecy more literally believe it does give a window for when Jesus might return. For them, the most salient point asserts that the second coming of Jesus may be witnessed by those who were alive near the time of modern Israel's founding. At least that generation, the Baby Boomers, will not "pass away" before his return. Accordingly, when the last of the Baby Boomers have passed on, either Jesus will have kept his word and returned to rule the earth, or he will have been posthumously exposed as a fraud. Many believe that at some point just down the road, we will have an answer. Jesus will either be King of Kings, or he will be thought of forevermore as someone who deceived countless millions. Time will tell, but that time is not far off.

Empty Promises

As the end approached, Jesus began making promises to his disciples regarding their futures. Once again, it centered on the timing of his return or second coming. In Matthew 16:28, Mark 9:1, and Luke 9:27, Jesus pledged to his twelve disciples: "Some who are standing here will not taste death before they see the Kingdom of God."

What Jesus was offering to his disciples is that he would return and set up his kingdom on Earth before some of them died. Since this didn't happen, and Jesus knew all along it wouldn't, it must be considered a deliberate falsehood. Considering the stress of his adverse circumstances, perhaps Jesus had become desperate, if not delusional. He may have been acting out of character. After all, these were the worst days of his life.

In a second attempt to keep the disciples in the game after his death, Jesus added another enticement: "In my Father's house [heaven] are many mansions: if it were not so, I would have told you. I go to prepare a place for you. And if I go and prepare a place for you, I will come again, and receive you unto myself; that where I am, you may be also" (John 14:2–3).

With this assurance, Jesus once again laid the groundwork for a second coming proposed to occur shortly after he ascended to heaven. Without question, Jesus baited the disciples with the promise that they would not die before his return. To sweeten the pot, he pledged to take them back to heaven, where they would be rewarded with mansions. The second scenario is different from the first. With the second promise, Jesus takes his followers back to heaven. With the previous promise, he advised them he would be returning to institute his kingdom on Earth. Noteworthy is that in either case, some are pardoned from death. I wonder if these followers felt duped when they realized Jesus was not coming back after all, and that the promises of mansions and reprieves from death were empty lies. If he lied to his faithful followers, why should anyone believe him now?

***

Commentary

As Jesus' ministry drew to a close, he began to realize that he would soon face the reality of it all. Either he had been successful in gathering followers, such that his cause had a large base of support—or he fell short in that regard and would lack the public consensus necessary to ascend to the messianic throne. He understood that a display of strength within the Jewish community would be imperative if he wanted to influence the Temple hierarchy.

Most of the support Jesus enjoyed originated with his assertion that he was the Messiah. The time was right prophetically, and the circumstances in Jerusalem, Judah, and Israel were primed for the new Davidic Dynasty. The Jewish population was eager for Jesus to make good on his bold messianic proclamation.

Jesus was aware that lack of support would leave him high and dry. If he was unable to apply pressure on the Temple authorities, he would be left out in the cold. But, if diplomacy was unsuccessful, Jesus was not afraid to use force in attempting a Temple coup. That is evidenced by his willful attempt to start a riot at the Temple courtyard. Alas, it seems there was not enough steam for Jesus to make things happen.

If all else failed, Jesus had two options. He could turn and walk away in shame, or he could submit to martyrdom. It is not clear at what point Jesus drew on his understanding of the Hebrew Bible and began to weave a plausible paradigm to explain what he was sent by God to do. What he came up with was admittedly brilliant.

He first selected a false metaphorical application of the suffering servant from Isaiah 53—the purpose being to propose substitutional sacrifice. Next, he chose the story of Abraham and Isaac to illustrate substitutional atonement. The father-son aspects of that passage also fit well with his "God the Father and Jesus the Son" dynamic. Then Jesus brazenly stole the thunder from King David and proclaimed that he, not David, was the Son of God. And finally, Jesus borrowed from the Davidic Covenant to create his own "new covenant." He mixed it all together and painted a picture that explicated his potential execution quite well.

With his bases covered, Jesus triumphantly entered Jerusalem on Palm Sunday. For Jews, this was the day they had longed for. Unfortunately, it did not take Jesus long to lose most of his initial support. By the end of the week, it was obvious that he was not the Messiah after all. Jewish joy turned to Jewish anger. The only support Jesus had at that point was for his crucifixion.

The Crucifixion

Jesus was no stranger to the Hebrew Temple authorities in Jerusalem. He kept Passover at the Temple every year beginning in childhood.[1] The Chief Priests, elders, and scribes came to know Jesus well. At some point, he was approved to teach in synagogues and speak in the Temple, which meant he held the position of rabbi. Good rapport initially existed between Jesus and the Temple authorities. At some point, Jesus and the Temple leadership seemed to have a falling out. It is not known why this was, but it likely had to do with Jesus' claim to being the Messiah. The Chief Priests and others surely must have considered it and were of the sincere conviction that it was a baseless claim.

    The Jewish leadership in the time of Jesus, and always, was theoretically appointed by Yahweh to oversee, guide, and instruct his people. One must assume that the will of God was carried out in matters of great importance. If believers profess that God intervenes in the lives of Christians today, then one must expect that he oversaw the affairs of his people in the time of Jesus. If Jesus was the true Messiah, Yahweh would have revealed it to the men he had placed in authority. The New Testament does not record a single angelic appearance announcing the birth of the Messiah, or of anything that regarded Jesus of Nazareth. Christianity portrays the Jewish religious authorities as scheming, self-righteous hypocrites. It is doubtful they were. Keep in mind that Jesus was attempting to overthrow their rule and change the foundations of Judaism. Perhaps the Pharisees were arrogant and the Sadducees overly protective of the law—but they were not evil. That Christianity vilifies them seems unfair. Jesus was a quick-tempered and rebellious troublemaker. It is unlikely God would ever have sent such a man.

---

[1] Fredriksen, "When Jesus Celebrated Passover."

In spite of his initial rejection, Jesus continued to recruit followers for the purpose of building support. He would need a consensus among the people in order to place pressure on the Jewish authorities. The master plan appeared to include a coup of the Hebrew hierarchy, if necessary. In other words, Jesus was prepared to lead a revolt that would overthrow the established religious order of the day. He would become the Messiah by force.

The Temple religious leaders therefore sought to prevent the potential disasters Jesus presented, by eliminating him. The fact that there was enormous antipathy between them only added fuel to the fire. The actual plan to remove Jesus was most likely initiated at Passover. His violent conduct in the Temple courtyard demonstrated a willingness to take his revolt to the next level. They had seen, and now feared, the threat he posed. They knew such a revolt would result in the deaths of many Jews.

The stage was set. By Passover week, Jesus must have sensed that he would *not* be the anointed Messiah. Without doubt, he understood the implications posed by two recent attempts to stone him. Both John 8:56–59 and John 10:30–33 record instances where Jesus was nearly killed by angry mobs at the Temple. Each time it was because he had hubristically *equated himself with God*. It was for this reason he had been accused of blasphemy. The aggrieved mood of the Jews moved his disciples to warn him about returning to the Temple.

Even so, Jesus was not deterred. His entourage left Bethany and headed toward the city. As they neared a small village situated just outside of Jerusalem, Jesus instructed two of his disciples to take a young donkey that was tied up there and to bring it to him. He then prepared to enter the city on the back of the donkey as prophesied in the Old Testament book of Zechariah and referenced in John 12:15: "Fear not daughter of Zion; Behold your King is coming, Lowly and riding on a donkey."

Word had spread that Jesus was on his way to Jerusalem. A crowd gathered at the eastern gate where it was anticipated he would enter. Tension filled the air. Everyone wondered what would happen. When he arrived, the crowd shouted, "Hosanna, blessed is the King of Israel!" They laid palm branches before him as he rode the donkey through the crowd. Part of the group that was gathered remained faithful to the idea that Jesus was their Messiah. Others had already cast off the notion that Jesus would liberate them from the rule of Rome. This had been the great hope of the people. Yet Jesus would fail them in a way that must have been crushing. It is clear that he played into this dramatic scene, not hesitating to take advantage of their enthusiasm. At least as regards the Messiah, it was all a cruel hoax—a hoax for which he would be crucified.

On Tuesday, Jesus went to the Temple and violently challenged the practice of currency exchange. Conjecture suspects he was attempting to get himself arrested so that his supporters would rise up and riot. He was not arrested, and no one protested.

The following day Jesus went to the Temple and was interrogated by the Pharisees. He gave clever but astute answers to several trick questions. He angrily criticized the Pharisees and the Sadducees for being "hypocrites and liars." Following his name-calling tirade, Jesus went to the Mount of Olives with the disciples. There he delivered warnings to Pharisees in the form of the "eight woes." Matthew recorded them in the twenty-third chapter of his Gospel. Each began with the phrase, "Woe unto you …!"

On Thursday night, Jesus met with his disciples for the Last Supper. It was there, in the upper room, that the Christian tradition of Holy Communion was instituted. Jesus described again how he was about to suffer, and once again spoke of the coming Kingdom of God. He maintained his soon-to-be-shed blood would represent his new covenant. Meanwhile, the disciples argued amongst themselves as to which of them should be considered the greatest. Their demeanor was unexpected. Was the gravity and meaning of Jesus' words lost on them? Jesus admonished the disciples and proceeded to reveal all that he had in store for them in his kingdom. At some point, Jesus mentioned that one of them would betray him. They all wondered aloud who it would be. Of course, it would be Judas Iscariot. In fact, he had already done so—or had he?

The Betrayal?

The Coptic Gospel of Judas was discovered in the late 1970s as part of a codex dating to the third century CE. It is believed to be a direct translation from a Greek text that predates the codex. This Gospel describes conversations between Jesus and Judas Iscariot that occurred just prior to the Passover when Jesus was crucified. In these conversations, it becomes apparent that Judas was a faithful follower of Jesus and that Jesus greatly trusted him. The lost Gospel of Judas bears witness to something completely different than what is recorded in the canonized Gospels. It relates that Jesus asked Judas to betray him so events would transpire as they were supposed to. In the key passage, Jesus tells Judas, "You will exceed all of them. For you will sacrifice the man who clothes me." It does not appear that Jesus considered it treason for Judas to betray him. Rather, it seems he viewed it as a duty that only Judas could accomplish. According to this account, Judas went to the Jewish chief priests and offered to tell them where Jesus would be. But he did so at the instruction of Jesus.[2]

The offer by Judas to betray Jesus was made two days before the actual event in the Garden of Gethsemane (Matt. 26:14–16). It seems there was some predetermined place and time for it to occur. On the night in question, Jesus did, in fact, wait at the Garden instead of proceeding on to Bethany where he had been staying. On that night, at the Last Supper, Jesus had instructed Judas to "go do what you must do, quickly" (John 13:27). The Greek word for betrayal, *paradidómi*, is also the same word used for "to hand over."[3] Indeed, it seems very unlikely that a faithful disciple of Jesus would sell him out for a few pieces of silver. If he did so, there would be an implication that Judas did not think Jesus was who he said he was. After all, who would betray someone whom they sincerely believed to be the Son of God? The more reasonable explanation is that the two of them agreed Judas would hand his master over to Jewish authorities in a prescribed fashion as determined in advance. It was to occur *after* Jesus erupted in the Temple courtyard so as to provide a reason for his arrest. However, the Temple authorities, though irritated by his disruptive behavior, were looking past that incident to a far more serious charge of blasphemy. Blasphemy was punishable by crucifixion.

---

[2] "The Lost Gospel of Judas" and "Gospel of Judas."
[3] Strong's Greek: 3860—paradidómi."

The canonized Gospels take the position that Judas was possessed by Satan. The supposition holds that for anyone to betray the real Messiah was an act that only the devil could orchestrate (see John 6:70–71). The biblical account further reports that Jesus knew Judas was a devil from the time he recruited him. If true, then it is a curiosity that Jesus was willing to partner with a demon-possessed follower. Assuming God's son would have keen foresight, the question arises: "Why would he purposely poison his ministry by recruiting a satanic disciple?" More likely, this accusation was added later in order to protect Jesus from looking oblivious. Yet another variation on this theme is that the devil came and went from Judas—once at the Last Supper, and before that, when he made his deal with the Chief Priests. It comes across as unlikely that a faithful follower of Jesus could be so easily possessed by the ultimate evil. It would be more logical to conclude that Satan's alleged involvement in the betrayal account was added to mitigate the issues posed in the above paragraph. In reality, it seems more likely that Judas Iscariot handed Jesus over as he had been instructed to, and that this was not a case of "the devil made me do it."

The Money Changers

In the period of the Second Temple, Jews who made the pilgrimage from far-off places traveled to Jerusalem to worship at Passover. Acts 2:5 describes that they came from "every nation under heaven." In fact, they likely came from Egypt in the south, Syria in the north, and from lands east of the Jordan River valley. These pilgrims brought considerable sums of foreign currency to spend while they were in Jerusalem. When these currencies involved the Temple authorities, who were responsible for depositing offerings in the Temple treasury, there was a requirement to convert the monies to a common currency. There was a need, therefore, for money exchangers who could handle these transactions. Additionally, there were those present who were offering animals for purchase that would be used for sacrifices. It was a system that made the workings of the Temple more efficient, especially for those who had traveled a great distance to get there.[4]

Mark 11:15–17 describes how Jesus entered the Temple courtyards and became infuriated at the sight of all this activity which was not directly involved with the spiritual essence of the Temple. He felt that it was a direct affront to God and that the money changers were a "den of thieves." His anger erupted into a furious and violent assault on all who were engaged in these ancillary activities. He whipped those who were involved, overturned the money exchange tables, and left the courtyards in upheaval. *He had known of this conduct within the Temple walls for the entirety of his life. Why now the overreaction?* It was described as a "cleansing." Nevertheless, a violent eruption should have been out of character for the Son of God. *Or was this possibly a well-thought-out way of "crossing the line" that would lead to his own arrest?* The scenario that Jesus was playing out points to the latter explanation.

The Garden

The next evening, Jesus went to the Garden of Gethsemane to pray. His demeanor was one of a man who knew the end was near. His prayers to God the Father reflected anxiety at the highest level. He even allegedly asked if *this cup* could pass by him. Jesus was so stressed by what he knew was about to transpire that, according to the 22nd chapter of the Gospel of Luke, he sweat blood: "And being in agony, He prayed more earnestly. Then His sweat became like great drops of blood falling to the ground" (Luke 22:44).

Luke was a physician. He was familiar with the condition that we know today as hematidrosis (sweating blood). It occurs only rarely and then only under circumstances of great stress. It is perhaps the most visible form of high anxiety.

An evangelical pastor once explained that anxiety is a sin. His rationale came from the book of Philippians where the Apostle Paul says, "Be anxious for nothing. But in all things, through prayer and supplication, make your requests be made known to God" (Phil. 4:6). To do other than this verse instructs, said the pastor, "is to

---

[4] "Money Changers."

violate the scripture, which is a sin." The pointed response he received went as follows: "If Jesus was so full of anxiety in the Garden that he sweat blood, you are unwittingly accusing him of sinning just before he was supposed to pay the price for the sins of the world." In all fairness, anybody who believes they are facing a brutal death would be wracked with fear, perhaps even the Son of God. Of course, Jesus was a mortal human like the rest of us. In that case, it should not be surprising that he was exhibiting signs of high anxiety.

After several hours of prayer, Jesus saw the soldiers approaching with Judas. Judas came to Jesus and kissed him. After a brief scuffle, the guards led Jesus away. The reports of the arrest in the Garden, as well as the discourse between Jesus and those who confronted him, vary from Gospel to Gospel but are reasonably consistent. One difference is that John's report specifies that those who arrested Jesus included Roman soldiers. The other Gospels stipulate that only Temple guards were part of the arresting party. At that point, the matter remained within the jurisdiction of Temple authorities. There was yet no reason for the Romans to be involved. Presumably, the arrest was part of a plan that would see Jesus taken into custody for his part in the Temple courtyard disturbance. Without the violent courtyard behavior, there was no basis in fact that would allow for Jesus to be arrested. Jesus himself questioned why he had not been arrested at the Temple. Supposition is, he expected to be arrested in front of a large crowd there, thus inciting a riot. Perhaps Jesus now believed he was headed to jail for his "cleansing" conduct. In truth, all the accusations that were ultimately forthcoming, relative to his crucifixion, were made after he was arrested. They centered on answers to questions that regarded his messianic claims, the most serious being that he had equated himself to God. At some point after his arrest, Jesus must have realized that he was headed for the cross.

Caiaphas along with the other priests and elders looked for reasons they could present to the Roman authority that would justify the crucifixion of Jesus. In the end, it was the charge of blasphemy that the Sanhedrin used to convict him. Pontius Pilate found nothing wrong with him (Luke 23:4). However, he had only considered Roman law in making that determination. He reluctantly acquiesced to the Hebrew claim that Jesus had violated Jewish law regarding blasphemy. Some expositors wrongly claim that Jesus was convicted of sedition or treason. There is nothing in scripture that says Jesus was executed for those reasons. In fact, it is clearly stated that Pilate found "nothing wrong with him."

While Jesus was being accused in front of Pilate, he answered nothing (Matt. 27:12). This was in keeping with the prophecy of Isaiah 53:7 where it says: "He was oppressed and afflicted, Yet he opened not his mouth; He was led as a lamb to the slaughter, and as a sheep before its shearers is silent, so he opened not his mouth."

During his interrogation by Pilate, Jesus continued his silence. In addition to blasphemy, there were other accusations raised by the Jewish religious leaders. Jesus refused to defend himself against any of them. Finally, Pilate asked him if he was the King of the Jews, to which he replied, "It is as you say." In a sarcastic gesture, Pontius Pilate had a sign nailed above Jesus on the cross. It read "INRI," an acronym for "Jesus of Nazareth, King of the Jews."

Pilate did what he could to avoid crucifying Jesus. He first sent him to be brutally and violently scourged, a fate that was in and of itself a horrible punishment. When that proved to be insufficient to satisfy the angry crowd, he offered to exchange Barabbas for Jesus. Barabbas was a thug who led a rebellion of his own which killed many. The crowd chose to have Barabbas released instead of Jesus. They came to see Jesus as an impostor and a betrayer. Their anger was steeped against the pretender who had apparently duped them. There was a great sense of disappointment that came with the understanding that Jesus was not going to rise up and repel the Romans from Judah. In light of this, there was nothing else Pilate could do, so he reluctantly capitulated and ordered Jesus crucified.

The Cross

The picture of the three crosses silhouetted against the sky on the hill of Golgotha is an iconic one. Jesus hung on the cross between two criminals. There are seven things that Jesus is reported to have said from the cross. Each Gospel offers up one or more of these phrases, but none reports all of them. They are:

1. "Father, forgive them for they know not what they do" (Luke 23:34).
2. "Truly, I say unto you [the criminal to his right], this day you will be with me in Paradise" (Luke 23:43).
3. [Speaking to his mother] "Woman behold your son." [Speaking to the Apostle John] "Behold your mother" (John 19:26–27).
4. "My God, my God, why have you forsaken me?" (Matt. 27:46 and Mark 15:34).
5. "I thirst" (John 19:28).
6. "It is finished" (John 19:30).
7. "Father into thy hand I commend my spirit" (Luke 23:46).

Only John was an actual eyewitness to the crucifixion. It is not certain why he did not report all seven phrases, but it may be that the additional phrases related by Matthew, Mark, and Luke were after-the-fact additions. The phrase, "My God, my God, why have you forsaken me?" is a direct quote from Psalm 22:1, which was written by David. It is the only phrase that both the Gospels of Matthew and Mark attribute to Jesus on the cross. Given the circumstances, it seems unlikely Jesus would borrow from the Psalms for the sake of being poetic. Then, when Jesus said to the thief on his right, "This day thou shalt be with me in Paradise," it is not clear whether Jesus was referencing Paradise, the Third Heaven, or Paradise in Sheol, otherwise known as Abraham's bosom. Christian denominations embrace different interpretations of this.

Dr. Bart Ehrman, distinguished professor of religious studies at the University of North Carolina, believes it is an error to conflate the four Gospel accounts in an attempt to resolve the contradictions. It is his position that each account should stand alone as the author's distinct message. He explains, "People don't realize that these are very different portrayals." He also relates how each depiction differs in what the author interprets the mind of Jesus to be thinking—how his words and demeanor reveal what he truly believes is his relationship to God the Father, and how he views his crucifixion.

For instance, Mark's account ends with a cry of dereliction, while Luke's account portrays Jesus as calm and in control.[5]

The end came at around 3:00 p.m. The time Jesus spent on the cross, approximately three hours, was far less than typical. Many took three days to die. Also, it was Roman custom to leave the body of the crucified on the cross indefinitely as a warning to others that Rome did not tolerate rebellion or lawlessness. It was unusual that the body of Jesus was taken down and given over to others who were outside of Roman authority. The Gospel of John reports that when the Roman soldiers came to break Jesus' legs, as was done to hasten death, it appeared he was already dead, so instead they put a spear into his side to ensure it. There are a handful of commentators who believe Jesus was supposed to survive the crucifixion and that the guard who speared him did so outside of a plan that was agreed to between Pilate and Joseph of Arimathea.

Joseph of Arimathea was a wealthy and politically connected member of the Jewish council. Some believe he was the uncle of Jesus. One way or another, he knew Jesus well enough to take responsibility for his burial. The pretext for the early removal of Jesus' body was consideration that it was Preparation Day, with the next day being the Passover. The Romans had never been concerned with such issues before, and it is unlikely that they would have consented under normal circumstances. The opinion that Jesus was supposed to survive the cross is, nevertheless, a completely speculative one. It is in keeping with prophecy, however, that the true Jewish Messiah was not foretold to be put to death.

The tomb where Joseph of Arimathea was believed to have laid the corpse of Jesus was in a garden near the hill of Golgotha. With the help of Nicodemus, another influential follower of Jesus, the body was placed in the tomb and then wrapped in linen. It was not treated with herbs and spices as is customary for the preparation of the deceased. There was no time for that and, according to custom, the preparation was done by females who were closest to the deceased. In this case, that would include Mary, the mother of Jesus, his sisters, and possibly Mary Magdalene. Nevertheless, *it must be asked why the body of Jesus would be prepared for burial*

---

[5] Ehrman, "Jesus and the Hidden Contradictions of the Gospels."

at all? If the people closest to him believed he would be resurrected, why would they bother to prepare him for burial? The fact that the three women closest to Jesus appeared Sunday morning to finish burial preparations, gives away that they were not sincere in expecting Jesus to rise up from the dead.

The Pharisees and Jewish elders had been worried that Jesus' followers might steal the body and claim that he had risen from the dead as he said he would. The elders allegedly approached Pontius Pilate and requested that the tomb be sealed, and a guard be posted for three days. At least, the Gospel of Matthew reports that this was the case. Mark, Luke, and John make no mention of it. Since it is doubtful that the tomb would have been ordered sealed before the body was fully prepared, Matthew's account lacks credibility. In addition, Matthew makes the claim that the guards were bribed by the Pharisees and instructed to say that the body was stolen while they slept (Matt. 28:11–15). This is highly unlikely, as the guards would have been at extreme risk for punishment, either for admitting they were asleep on the job, or worse, that they had taken a bribe to lie to their superiors. While Matthew attempts to cover all the bases, his story is more than likely embellishment or fabrication, as that was his style.

Zombies for Jesus

Matthew further reports that immediately following the last cry of Jesus from the cross, a large earthquake tore the veil of the Temple in two. This represented, so say Bible scholars, the ending of the Old Covenant. No longer were Jews separated from God by the veil that isolated the Holy of Holies from the sanctuary. It is considered to represent the restoration of direct communion between God and man. Matthew then reports on other events resulting from the earthquake. "And the earth quaked, and the rocks were split, and the graves were opened; and many bodies of the saints who had died, were raised; and coming out of the graves after His resurrection, they went into the holy city and appeared to many" (Matt. 27:51–53).

This seemingly tongue-in-cheek passage prompts skeptical readers to scratch their heads and possibly even chuckle. It appears to be written in jest. Serious students of scripture are being asked to believe that "many bodies" arose from their graves, went into Jerusalem, and witnessed for Jesus. It certainly creates an image that would make for a good "walking dead" movie in today's world. One must wonder what the reaction of the populace was. If formerly dead people were descending on the city, a typical reaction would be to run, not stay put and talk with them! Extra-biblical references to zombies, in this context or any other, have not been uncovered. This event surely would have been of historical significance. None of the Roman or Jewish historians writes a single word regarding it. *It is astonishing that under the doctrine of biblical inerrancy, Christians are compelled to believe and defend that this fanciful event truly happened.*

Historical Fact or Fiction?

With respect to the crucifixion itself, there exists only a single extra-biblical reference to it. Roman historian Josephus, in his *Antiquities,* is alleged to have written: "He led away many Jews, and also many of the Gentiles. He was the so-called Christ. When Pilate, acting on information supplied by the chief men around us, condemned him to the cross, those who had attached themselves to him at first, did not cease to cause trouble."[7]

This short reference to the crucifixion is widely considered to be from an altered source. Literary historians familiar with Josephus' writing are universally convinced that it does not appear to be written in the style of Josephus.

There is no other historical record of the crucifixion of Jesus, or even of Jesus himself, that is contemporary to the time in which he lived. The crucifixion account of the Apostle John is the only account written from near the time period in which it is alleged to have occurred. It is not known how many years after the events actually happened that John wrote his account.

Three Days and Three Nights?

During his ministry, Jesus had mentioned that he would be in the "belly of the earth" for "three days and three nights." His body was placed in a tomb before sunset following his Friday afternoon crucifixion and just prior to the Sabbath. He was interred until his body was discovered missing at sunrise on the first day of the week, or Sunday. This means he *only remained among the dead for thirty-six hours or less. The Hebrew day begins at sunset, so it follows that Jesus was in the tomb for one Hebrew day and one additional night. Three days would extend from Friday at sunset until Monday at sunset.* Is there any viable explanation for this discrepancy?

Ordinarily, one might expect that anticipation over Jesus' self-prophesied resurrection would bring his followers to the tomb on the third day, or Monday. If the intention of his disciples was to steal away Jesus' body and claim he was risen from the dead, they probably had to consider a way to do it before a crowd of onlookers gathered on Monday. Therefore, they may have taken his body early.

Another somewhat improbable scenario is that Jesus survived the crucifixion. There are those who claim he did not die on the cross. Even Pilate appeared to be surprised when he heard that Jesus had died so soon (Mark 15:16). The theory proposes that Jesus intended to fake his own death. Perhaps to impart endurance, some type of drug had been given via the sponge that was put to his mouth after he uttered, "I thirst." Hypothetically, he may have been given a mixture of belladonna and opium to dull his pain and sedate him. An even more audacious proposal suggests that a deathlike state was induced using an exotic potion such as tetrodotoxin.[6] Whatever it was, it worked quickly—Jesus appeared to expire soon after drinking from the sponge that was elevated to his mouth. Regardless of what transpired, if Jesus survived the cross, it would be necessary to get him to a place of recovery as soon as it could be accomplished. Because of that, his body was removed from the tomb prior to the three full days that Jesus predicted he would be among the dead.

Christian crucifixion dogma attempts to excuse the inconsistency with prophecy by offering that credit for an entire day should be given to the Friday afternoon of the crucifixion (Good

---

[6] Yang, "Tetrodotoxin" and Wilson, "How Zombies Work."
[7] "Antiquities," Book 18, Chapter 3, Part 3.

Friday). Assignment of a complete day is then afforded to the few hours that passed from the cross until sundown. There is no argument that Passover Saturday should receive allowance for being a whole day. But an entire day's credit for the few hours of darkness that occurred on the first day of the week is a significant overreach. Instead of stating that Jesus was dead for three days and three nights, as he foretold in Matthew 12:40, it is more common to hear of him rising "on the third day." Semantics are cleverly employed to resolve the discrepancy between prophecy and what truly occurred. It is also possible that subsequent contributors to the Gospels retrospectively changed "three days and three nights" to "on the third day" as another way of resolving the mistake.

***

Commentary

The crucifixion of Jesus of Nazareth marks a milestone moment in the timeline of human history. Yet were it not for the biblical accounts, we would never have known of it. For that matter, we would never have known of Jesus, either.

The more the crucifixion and the events leading up to it are scrutinized, it becomes clearer that Jesus' popularity had substantially waned by the time of the Passover. He had already come to realize that being the Messiah was not going to occur unless violence was involved.

In many of his conversations, Jesus is found leaning heavily on the "works" (miracles) he has performed in making the case he is God incarnate. Giving some thought to that, it seems he could have gone much further in making a convincing argument.

God allegedly performed some exceedingly spectacular feats—all recorded in the Hebrew Bible. Consider these: The Mount Carmel sacrifice occurred to prove that the God of Israel was the true God. God brought the ten plagues upon Egypt to prove to the Pharoah that he was "mighty God." Yahweh parted the Red Sea, split the Jordan River, brought down the walls of Jericho—and much more. It is safe to say that monumental miracles accomplished God's purpose.

Jesus talked about moving mountains by having the faith of a mustard seed. So why did he fail to think big, himself? Jesus steadfastly refused to utilize "on demand" miracles for the purpose of proving who he was. He refused Satan in that regard. He likewise rejected requests from his brothers to prove himself by doing the works he was said to have done. Their sentiment is expressed in John 7:4 where they admonish him, saying: "For no one does anything in secret while he himself seeks to be known openly. If you do these things, you show yourself to the world."

Following his heavenly father's example does not amount to braggadocio. Instead of revealing the glory of God to the masses, it tells one and all that he would not, because he could not. His lack of moxie in saving himself from crucifixion underscored that Jesus of Nazareth was an impostor, an impostor for the ages. This reinforces the need to rethink the Jesus you thought you knew.

8

Is He Risen?

Virtually every New Testament scholar emphasizes the importance of the resurrection to the Christian faith. It is considered a central tenet, without which Christ's victory over sin would not have been accomplished. Theologically, the resurrection validated that Jesus was a deity and underscored the message of hope he delivered during his ministry on Earth. If there had been no resurrection, the power of the Gospel would have been deflated and emptied of its credibility. More than likely, Jesus would have faded into history and been forgotten. Thus, the resurrection is the key that unlocked the door to his purpose and gave his church staying power.

If it could be demonstrated that the resurrection of Jesus was invented, then all biblical dogma that relies on it would become *falsum doctrinam*. The governing control exerted by a central tenet is undermined by any *false doctrine* that serves as its foundational support. Such a circumstance invokes the Latin idiom *falsus in uno, falsus in omnibus*—false in one thing, false in everything. Since doctrines are nigh unto immutable, a new biblical finding, or an invalidating event, would be necessary to overturn one. Exposing that the resurrection of Jesus Christ was chicanery would accomplish just that. Subsequently, Jesus would fall from grace, his legacy downgraded to that of just another garden-variety martyr. The religious institution known as Christianity would crumble.

In this chapter and the next, we will take a look at potentially incriminating textual evidence that suggests the resurrection scenario was carefully planned with the intent of creating a monumental deception. Insight gained by comparison of the Gospel accounts might at least open some eyes to the possibility of a mortal Jesus. Care has been taken to avoid conflating the four Gospel narratives into a single unified anecdote so that the integrity of each writer's perspective is preserved. A comparative criticism of the resurrection stories will highlight the notable irregularities and contradictions found there. Whether the findings point to a counterfeit resurrection is for readers to decide for themselves.

Matthew

At dawn on the first day of the week (Sunday following the Sabbath), Jesus' mother Mary and his close follower Mary Magdalene appeared at the tomb. Matthew does not indicate if the women were there in expectation of seeing the risen Jesus, or for the purpose of finalizing the preparation of the body for burial. (Joseph of Arimathea had only wrapped it in linen.) Matthew relates that the angel who had rolled away the stone was seen sitting upon it when the women arrived. The angel invited them to view the place where Jesus had lain. He then told them, "He is not here; for He is risen." Following that, the angel said Jesus was "going before them into Galilee" and that they should go back and tell the disciples the good news. But before they can get back to the place where they were all staying, Jesus intercepted them and said, Rejoice! They fell down and grabbed Jesus around his feet and proceeded to worship him. He instructed them to go and tell my brethren to go to Galilee, and there they will see me (Matt. 28:10).

Later in this passage are two verses of some interest. Matthew 28:16–17 says: "Then the eleven disciples went away into Galilee, to the mountain that Jesus had appointed for them. When they saw Him, they worshiped Him…*but some doubted*".

Mark

The Gospel of Mark recounts how Mary Magdalene, Mary the mother of James, and Salome came to Jesus' tomb at sunrise on the first day of the week. *They brought spices in order to prepare the body.* The question was raised as to who would roll the stone away for them. When they approached the tomb, they found that the stone had already been rolled away. All three entered the tomb and found "a young man clothed in a long white robe sitting on the right side" (Mark 16:6). This young man, not identified as an angel, told them that Jesus was risen. He is not here. See the place where they laid him. The women were then instructed to go tell His disciples, and Peter, that He is going before you to Galilee; there you will see him, as He said to you. The frightened women fled the tomb. Mark 16:8 reports that they "said nothing to anyone."

This would seem to be a complete account of what occurred, as reported by Mark. However, Mark then recapitulated his account in a much different way. The puzzling second account, which immediately follows the first one, tells how Jesus was resurrected early on the first day of the week and appeared to Mary Magdalene. There is no indication given that she had any interaction with him. It records how she ran back to the others and told them that she had seen Jesus. Mark 16:11 says, "And when they heard that He was alive and had been seen by her, *they did not believe*" (emphasis mine). Their disbelief revealed that they had enormous doubt regarding Jesus' authenticity. Clearly, they were not expecting a resurrection.

Luke

The version of the resurrection found in the Gospel of Luke differs from the others. Luke describes that the women who had come with him from Galilee…and certain other women came to the tomb *bringing burial spices they had prepared*. This indicates the task they were there to perform. Luke 24:10 specifically gives the names of Mary Magdalene, Joanna, Mary the mother of James, as well as "other women…" They also found the stone rolled away and went into the tomb. They could not find the body of Jesus "and were perplexed." Suddenly, "Two men stood by them in shining garments" (Luke 24:4). These men said, "He is not here, but is risen!" One of the men was dismayed that the women had forgotten what Jesus had foretold regarding his crucifixion and resurrection. Then all the women returned from the tomb and reported all these things to the eleven and to all the rest. Luke 24:11 says, "And their words seemed to them like idle tales, and they did not believe them." Despite the disbelief, the Apostle Peter arose and ran to the tomb. There he saw the linen cloths lying by themselves. No one appeared to him, and he left, "marveling to himself at what had happened."

Again, direct scriptural reporting depicts skeptical disciples who seemed perplexed by the notion of miraculous resurrection.

John

In the version found in John 20, Mary Magdalene went to the tomb early, while it was still dark. She may have gone early while the air was still cool. Tombs are like ovens. As the outside temperature goes up, the tombs get hot. Adding in the fetid smell of a decaying corpse makes it understandable why getting to the tomb early was important. Mary was not there seeking to be the first to see the risen Christ.

As in the other accounts, Mary saw that the stone was not covering the entrance to the tomb. She is said to have fled and then come across Simon, Peter and John somewhere, but it does not say where. Mary told them, "They have taken the Lord out of the tomb, and we do not know where they have laid Him." (The pronoun "we" is used even though Mary Magdalene is identified as being the only one who went to the tomb.) Mary's words imply she had not even considered that Jesus was risen. Peter and John both ran to the tomb from wherever they had been. John is said to have outrun Peter and to have arrived at the tomb first. He did not go in; rather, he stooped down and looked inside. He saw the linen cloths lying there. Then Peter arrived and went into the tomb. John 20:6–7 says,

> And he saw the linen cloths lying there, and the handkerchief that had been around His head, not lying with the linen cloths, but folded together in a place by itself.

According to John 20:8–10, "The other disciple [John] went in also, and he saw and believed. For as yet they did not know the Scripture that He must rise again from the dead." Note that the disciples were not apprised by an angel that Jesus was risen. But perhaps of greater importance is that John writes of the disciples' lack of awareness regarding his resurrection. However, Matthew 16:21; 17:23; 20:18–19, Mark 9:31, and Luke 24:46 tell of Jesus instructing his disciples that he will be crucified and will rise on the third day. Therefore, how is it conceivable that the Apostle John, and the other disciples, did not anticipate that Jesus would be resurrected?

Luke's account reflects that the women at the tomb had forgotten Jesus' prophetic words regarding his resurrection. Thus, they had failed to remember the pinnacle event of Jesus' ministry. Was that indeed the case, or had they never truly been made aware in the first place? These ambiguous circumstances represent glaring textual inconsistencies. Then ask the question once again: "Why was Jesus being prepared for burial when he had allegedly declared numerous times that he would be resurrected in three days?" With that, the quizzical nature of the story amplifies. It provides even more evidence that the scriptures are lacking in coherency on critical issues and casts greater doubt on their authenticity.

In John's resurrection account, Mary Magdalene is said to have entered the tomb after the disciples reportedly went away again to their own homes. There she saw two angels in white sitting, one at the head and the other at the foot, where the body of Jesus had lain (John 20:12). When Mary told them she did not know where they had taken the body of the Lord, a voice from behind her said, Woman, why are you weeping? Whom are you seeking? (John 20:15). She turned around and saw Jesus. However, *she did not recognize him*. She had supposed that he was the gardener. She was seeking a deceased Jesus, not a risen one. Not until Jesus called her name did she realize it was him. She then said, Rabboni! (teacher). Jesus told her not to touch him as he had not yet ascended to My Father. Ironically, Jesus would subsequently invite doubting Thomas to put his fingers into the wounds that the nails had made and into his side where the spear had pierced. Think back to the account Matthew gave and recall that Mary Magdalene and Mary the mother of Jesus fell down and wrapped their arms around the feet of Jesus. Hence, Gospel accounts differ with regard to physical contact made with Jesus.

Will the Real Resurrection Account Please Stand Up?

Reviewing the four accounts of the resurrection yields *four different descriptions* of what transpired. There are four versions of who appeared at the tomb. There are four versions of who was seen there—one angel, one young man, two men, and then two angels. Where these individuals appeared is different. What was said is similar but far from identical. Jesus appeared to:

1. Mary Magdalene and Mary the mother of Jesus
2. Mary Magdalene without interaction,
3. Nobody
4. Mary Magdalene with discourse.

These inconsistencies are important given the magnitude of the resurrection. They add to the entirety of incoherence that is the Gospel message.

***

Commentary

Christian commentary nearly always misrepresents the purpose for which the women appeared at the tomb on Sunday morning. Yet, the Bible's own words indicate clearly that they had prepared spices and were there to complete burial preparations on the body of Jesus. The women closest to Jesus did not arrive at dawn expecting to see the risen Christ. The implication derived from the biblical text is that they were not anticipating a resurrection. Nor were the disciples. There is an explicit lack of awareness expressed by both John and Luke with regard to a resurrected Christ. Perhaps that explains why "they did not believe."

The conflict appears to originate with differences between alleged pre-crucifixion Bible passages and post-crucifixion scriptural reports. Alleged, because there are verses that appear to have been inserted after the fact for the purpose of creating a false picture—one that endeavors to portray the crucifixion and resurrection events as being synchronized by near-future prophecy. A more considered and rational explanation proposes that Jesus was crucified for equating himself to God and for hoaxing his standing as the Messiah. For doing so, he absorbed the full wrath of a jilted Jewish populous who felt conned and betrayed. He died on the cross of Calvary and was carted off to a tomb where burial preparations were initiated but not completed. He was in the tomb for one day and one night following the crucifixion. The alleged post-crucifixion appearances of Jesus generated skepticism and disbelief. None of what happened equates to "God's plan for humankind." It is more properly described as predictable real-time behavior given the circumstances.

To believe Jesus resurrected himself is to ignore the palpable lack of credibility attributed to the Bible's own incoherent accounts. Thankfully, most of the close followers of Jesus seemed to report consistently regarding their initial disbelief. Beyond that, each Gospel author, and others who followed, laid down their own agenda-laced versions as seen from each one's unique perspective. However, facts are facts. Certainly, eyewitness accounts sometimes vary. Nevertheless, it is important that reports are consistent so that the depth and clarity of truth overcomes all doubt. Here, once again, the Bible has fallen short of its obligation to provide us with consistency and transparency.

Post-Resurrection Appearances and the Ascension

In considering the accounts of Jesus' post-crucifixion appearances, it should be remembered that the Gospels of Matthew, Luke, and John were most likely written after the book of Mark. However, there is no consensus among Bible scholars regarding that. Others believe Matthew's Gospel was the first written. The Gospel of Mark was written by John Mark, a nephew of Barnabas, a colleague of the Apostle Paul. The book of Mark was not written by the Apostle Mark, also known as St. Mark, and it does not represent an eyewitness account. Bible scholars generally consider that it was written somewhere around the middle of the first century and no later than the destruction of Jerusalem in 70 CE. The other Gospels were most likely written near the end of the first century, closer to 90 CE. The Gospel of Mark may have provided the inspiration for the other three Gospels, which borrow from and expand on Mark's writing.

The original book of Mark ended at chapter sixteen, verse 8. There was a later addition following the original writing that extended the Gospel by ten verses. These ten verses contain Mark's (or someone's) account of Mary Magdalene's appearance at the tomb, the appearance of Jesus on the road to Emmaus, the account of Jesus giving the "great commission," and a single-verse mention of the ascension. The description of the ascension is so brief that it yields the impression of being a footnote. Since it was not mentioned at all in the original text, some believe that Jesus did not ascend to heaven but died on the cross or sometime soon after. Likewise, Mark's original Gospel text does not include an appearance of Jesus after he was allegedly resurrected. Originally, the final verse told of how the women (Mary Magdalene, Mary the mother of Jesus, and Salome) fled after being at the tomb, and how they told no one of the message that Jesus was risen. The fact that someone went back and added to this Gospel is suspicious, especially in light of the lengthier accounts of the post-resurrection period given in the subsequent Gospels. It is as if someone felt it was necessary to update the book of Mark with embellishments so it would be consistent with accounts that were written later.

There are well-defined differences between the Gospels with respect to the details of Jesus' appearances. This may be due to the fact that they did not have Mark to borrow from, at least as originally written. Otherwise, information transmitted orally, may have come from diverse sources that did not entirely agree. What follows is an accounting of the reported appearances of Jesus and brief comments on his ascension.

Matthew

According to Matthew, the resurrected Jesus appeared to Mary Magdalene and "the other" Mary after they left the tomb. Matthew is alone in reporting that Jesus spoke to the eleven remaining disciples at the mountain where he had sent them in Galilee. *Matthew conspicuously fails to mention the ascension.*

Mark

The original version of Mark did not include any mention of the ascension. A one-verse report of it was added at some later date, possibly by Mark, but most likely by someone else. With respect to appearances, Jesus appeared to Mary Magdalene soon after he arose, but there are no details given as to where. Following that, there is a mention of his appearance "in another form" to two followers as "they went into the country." Finally, he appeared to the eleven remaining disciples and gave the message of the great commission. Mark 16:19 describes that Jesus "was received up into heaven, and sat down at the right hand of God."

Luke

The first reported post-resurrection appearance of Jesus in the Gospel of Luke occurred on the road to Emmaus. This is the same appearance as the *two followers* mentioned in Mark. Jesus appeared "in another form" (Mark 16:12) on the road, where he encountered the two followers. One of them, Cleopas, was his uncle, the brother of Joseph. *Neither of the men recognized him,* even as they walked along and talked with him about the death of Jesus in Jerusalem.

Down the road, the two men reached their destination and invited Jesus to have dinner with them. Even then, "they did not recognize him" until he blessed the bread and then broke it. Immediately upon breaking the bread, Jesus vanished. At that point, they determined that it *must* have been *the Lord.* The account in Luke 24 says, "Their eyes were opened and they knew him." Frequently, the fact that these men do not recognize Jesus is glossed over or dismissed as unimportant. In reality, it deserves a better explanation than that. What is the significance of the dubious mention that he was in another form? Why would Jesus conceal his identity from them? How is it that someone's eyes can be *closed* to what they are seeing? What is the point of concealing who you are, only to disappear after revealing yourself?

The road to Emmaus is not the only account where the post-resurrected Jesus was not recognized. Some to whom he is alleged to have revealed himself to were perplexed. Jesus did not seem to look quite like himself. There are a few awkward explanations as to why that may have been. One offering is that Jesus was in his glorified body and that he looked different in that transmuted state. Some are convinced he was a spirit. But Bible scholars are adamant that Jesus was *not* a spirit after he rose from the dead. Skeptics have proposed that Jesus had a look-alike double who masqueraded as *the Lord* to a select few. There is even the unlikely theory that Jesus had a twin brother who replaced him after the crucifixion. All of this seems a bit fantastical. Perhaps the most likely explanation is that the alleged resurrection never occurred, and that accounts professing that it did happen were simply added to the Gospels at a later date.

There is also some question as to why the disciples remained in Jerusalem. Why had they not left for Galilee as Jesus had instructed them? (Matthew indicates they did, so there is a discrepancy.) Perhaps they were still not convinced that Jesus had risen from the dead and, therefore, did not want to travel to Galilee unnecessarily. In the upper room, where they hid, Jesus appeared in their midst and said, "Peace be with you." After seeing his wounds, Luke 24:41 says, "They still did not believe." At that point, Jesus led the disciples to nearby Bethany, blessed them, and ascended to heaven. His ascension is described in a single, somewhat indifferent, sentence (Luke 24:51).

John

The Gospel of John tells of the appearance of Jesus to Mary Magdalene in the tomb. Next, it reports that Jesus, the same evening as his resurrection, appeared to the disciples in the locked room where they were hiding. This is the same appearance mentioned in Luke. However, reading the text reveals an entirely different conversation. Eight days later, Jesus returned to the upper room and confronted Thomas, who continued to doubt. After seeing the wounds in Jesus' hands and feet, Thomas relents and decides to believe.

John 20:30–31 appears to be a closing passage. It ends the twentieth chapter with, "Jesus did many other signs in the presence of his disciples, which are not written in this book. But these are written that you may believe that Jesus is the Christ…" However, even though this passage appears to bring an end to the book of John, John 21 continues by describing an appearance Jesus made to the disciples at the Sea of Tiberias.

Upon arriving, Jesus found that most of the disciples had settled back into their former routines, of which fishing was primary. Again, on this day *Jesus was not recognized*, at least from afar. While the disciples fished, Jesus approached on the shore. They had not caught anything, so Jesus told them to cast their nets on the other side of the boat. Doing so, they caught so many fish that the boat was nearly swamped. It was following this, while eating breakfast, that Jesus admonished Peter for "not tending my sheep." Peter would go on to fulfill his responsibility to be "the rock on which Jesus would build his church" (Matt. 16:18).

This story may have been inserted by John to depict how the apostles were initially reluctant to make commitments regarding the Church and its ministry. Their hesitation possibly belied a continued skepticism that Jesus had been resurrected.

Of significance is that the Apostle John did not report anything of relevance regarding the ascension of Jesus. There is only a vague and ambiguous reference to a comment Jesus made to Peter. The comment implied that John would not die before Jesus returned. (John 21:22–23). Still, there is no mention of where Jesus was going. It is noteworthy that the comment Jesus made proved to be untrue. There is no explanation as to why John, "the one who Jesus loved," did not finish his report on the ministry of Jesus by including a description of his ascent into heaven.

Paul

Not mentioned so far is the Apostle Paul, the fervent convert to Christ who would come to zealously lead the charge in the years following the ministry of Jesus. Some have said that Paul changed the direction of Christianity by promoting the doctrine of grace. He was also largely responsible for expanding the Jesus movement by offering Gentiles the chance to participate. In doing so, he began to lay the groundwork for replacement theology.

In terms of his conversion and ministry, Paul came on the scene shortly after the crucifixion of Jesus. He was primarily an evangelistic missionary and a founder of churches. Even though he post-dates Jesus, Paul reported on the ascension in some detail. The book of Acts reports on a conversation Jesus had with his disciples just prior to his alleged ascent into heaven. It was during this dialogue that Jesus was asked by his disciples, "Lord, will You at this time restore the Kingdom of Israel?" (Acts 1:6). The question is meaningful as it reveals that the disciples remained under the impression that Jesus was the Messiah. In spite of his wholesale rejection by Jewish religious leaders, and Jews in general, did Jesus still intend to move forward with his messianic claim? This would seem to be an appropriate question and expectation. However, Jesus responded by saying, "It is not for you to know times or seasons which the Father has put in His own authority" (Acts 1:7). (Christian theology uses this verse to support the contention that Jesus would return from Heaven as the Messiah at some unknown time). Jesus then commissioned the disciples to be witnesses for him in all the world. In other words, Jesus told them bluntly, "It is none of your business when the Kingdom will come about. Just go out and tell the world about me." At that point, Paul alleges that Jesus was taken up into the clouds and out of sight. His description of the ascension seems terse and offhand. His cavalier attitude is not fitting in light of the magnitude of the event. Paul is well known for being verbose and descriptive. He made no effort to describe the ascension in vivid detail or to discuss its significance.

In his first letter (epistle) to the Church at Corinth, Paul proclaimed that Jesus was buried, and rose again on the third day "according to the Scriptures." Then he wrote: "He was seen by Cephas, then by the twelve. After that, He was seen by over five hundred brethren at once, of whom the greater part remain to the present, but some have died. After that He was seen by James and all the apostles" (I Cor. 15:5–7). Paul also reports how it was the risen Jesus who appeared to him after the crucifixion on the road to Damascus. However, Paul did not actually *see* Jesus. What he *did* see was a blinding light. Paul's sincere belief that he had encountered the risen Jesus is based on the voice he heard coming from the light and what it said to him. This was the time and place of Paul's conversion to Christianity.

The contention that Jesus made an appearance to over 500 brethren is sometimes disputed. Acts 1:9, 14–15 and 22 mention that only 120 brethren met together in Jerusalem at the time of his ascension. Likewise, the number 500 does not fit well with Acts 10:40–42, which says, "God raised Him up on the third day, and showed Him openly, not to all the people, but to witnesses chosen before God, even to us who ate and drank with Him after He arose from the dead." This verse is referencing the apostles and only the closest of Jesus' followers. Although Paul includes himself, his presence is not compatible with the post-resurrection timeline. Hence, the claim by Paul is at least an exaggeration and, at worst, a fabrication.

Although discrepancies regarding the life of Jesus abound throughout the Gospels, it is especially true where the post-crucifixion storyline is involved. Why is this so? One suggestion that comes to mind involves the process that saw the Gospels created. Obviously, this would include the original authorship. But translation, witness testimony, cultural bias, motivations, and oral tradition likewise play roles in how the Gospels were written. Perhaps a brief historical examination and background on the origins of each Gospel is indicated.

The Gospel According to Matthew

Matthew was one of the twelve disciples of Jesus. Bible scholars place the writing of his Gospel before the destruction of the Temple in 70 CE. Scholars who are versed in the historicity of the Bible tend to place the initial appearances of Matthew's Gospel later than that. Accusations include that the later dates change prophecy into history by taking advantage of a retrospective view. Matthew indulged himself with a prophetic fixation. He clearly took advantage of his own backward view of the events surrounding Jesus' life and ministry. In fact, if all of the Gospels were written years after Jesus was gone, then each of them would essentially represent backdated accounts. Backdated or not, there is still no explanation for why Matthew failed to mention the ascension.

Matthew was born in the first century, making him younger than Jesus. He was a tax collector by vocation. It is not known precisely when he died. One popular theory is that he was martyred in Ethiopia, where he was a missionary. This version relates he was impaled and beheaded. Matthew's primary audience was the Jewish population.

The Gospel According to Mark

Mark was written by John Mark, a colleague of the Apostle Paul. Mark accompanied his uncle Barnabas and Paul on their first missionary journey. However, he did not complete the journey, which led to his falling out with Paul and Barnabas. There is more support among scholars for a mid-first century appearance of

Mark's Gospel than for a much later date. His target audience appears to have been Roman. Though there were Romans who were Jews, most were not. They were therefore non-Jews, otherwise known as Gentiles.

Mark's Gospel omits the birth and childhood of Jesus. That he failed to initially include the ascension at the end of Mark 16 is truly noteworthy. The later addition of another ten verses is suspect. Like Luke and Paul, Mark's report on the ascension, originally missing, amounts to one brief sentence. For many, these curt, almost cavalier comments seem to diminish the importance of the ascension. Indeed, they come close to yielding an impression that there was no ascension.

The Gospel According to Luke

It is well known that Luke was a physician, but few realize he was a Greek physician. He was, in fact, a Gentile. Hence, much of his writing is directed toward Gentiles. Luke died in 84 CE; his date of birth is not known. There is a lack of evidence to support that he was actually the author of the book of Luke, and there continues to be scholarly debate about it. Much of Luke's Gospel is devoted to the post-resurrection period. He describes interactions between the resurrected Jesus and others in more detail than other authors do. To his credit, he is diligent in highlighting that, after the crucifixion, Jesus was not recognized by people who knew him. Luke does not appear to question that circumstance, nor does he try to explain why Jesus looks different. He simply throws it out for others to ponder.

The Gospel According to John

John, who refers to himself as "the one who Jesus loved," was the son of Zebedee, husband of Jesus' aunt Salome. John was therefore Jesus' cousin. Being born in 16 CE, he was significantly younger than Jesus. He died in 100 CE at age eighty-four. John is considered an eyewitness to the events recorded in his Gospel, which he wrote in the late first century. We have already discussed the bewildering fact that John did not mention the ascension. Nor does he record relevant events leading to it. Of the four Evangelists, John would otherwise seem to be the most likely to have expounded on it.

The Acts of the Apostles-Paul

The Apostle Paul has already been reviewed in some detail. He co-authored the book of Acts and wrote the book of Romans. The remainder of his New Testament contributions were the epistles—letters to various churches and individuals. Paul wrote primarily to Gentiles and championed the doctrine of grace. Following Jesus' death, he became a church founder and later a missionary. He is alleged to have died in Rome after Nero ordered the deaths of Christians.

***

Commentary

The post-resurrection ascension of Jesus to Heaven is mentioned in only two of the four Gospels. One of those Gospels only includes a brief mention of it that was added at a later date. The Apostle Paul penned a brief account that seems to be clouded by embellishment as well as questions regarding his standing as an eyewitness. The wheres and whens of Jesus' post-crucifixion appearances also vary significantly within the Gospels. For the most part, believers are willing to look past these discrepancies. Skeptics find the acceptance of the resurrection and the ascension of Jesus to be fanciful overreaches for which there is a paucity of reliable substantiation in the scriptures or elsewhere.

    The most salient points in this chapter are important ones. That Jesus was not recognized by followers after his alleged resurrection is of prime significance. The Bible gives no direct explanation. All one can do is speculate, and speculation leads to doubt. The preponderance of evidence points to the logical conclusion that the person of Jesus was not seen after he was crucified. Either a look-alike double appeared to a limited number of people or his appearances were deceptively written into the biblical text. Perhaps the fact that most solidifies New Testament malfeasance is that Jesus made repeated comments regarding his *soon return*. He did not return, and that should settle the matter of who he was.

"Post-Resurrection Appearances and the Ascension" concludes our review of the life of Jesus. We will now take a look at some interesting secondary aspects of his life. We will explore where he might have been buried, what he may actually have looked like, and whether or not he was married.

The Talpiot Tomb

In 1980 and 1981, during the construction of an apartment building in the eastern Jerusalem neighborhood of Talpiot, a construction crew uncovered two tombs that dated to the time of Jesus. In one of the tombs, ten bone boxes, or ossuaries, were found. Six were inscribed with names, the most notable being "Jesus, son of Joseph." Other boxes were inscribed with the names of people associated with the family of the biblical Jesus. Intense debate erupted when it was suggested that this may be the family tomb of Jesus of Nazareth.

The tomb is thought to have been buried by the great Jerusalem earthquake of 363 CE. When discovered, it was partially filled with a red clay-like mud. In addition, three skulls were found on the floor of the tomb, arranged in a triangle that pointed toward the Temple.

The Hebrew burial custom of the time in which Jesus lived was a two-part process. The first part involved laying the deceased on a tomb slab. After rubbing the body with spices (aloe and myrrh), a linen burial cloth, or shroud, was wrapped around the body. The body remained in place for two or three months or until the soft tissues had decomposed, leaving only bones. At that point, the bones were placed in an ossuary and interred either in a family tomb or in a solitary tomb, depending on the circumstances. This method of burial was used from about 20 BCE. until 70 CE.

Much is known about the family of Jesus. He had four brothers, or half-brothers, depending on your point of view, and at least two sisters, Anna and Salome. The names of those mentioned in the tomb are:

Yeshua bar Yosef (*Jesus, son of Joseph*). The inscription on this ossuary is difficult to read. Indeed, another possible rendering of the inscription may be "Hunan" instead of Yeshua.

However, with another of the ossuaries reading "Yehuda bar Yeshua," it is far more likely that the inscription reads "Jesus." A shard was found near the Yeshua ossuary that contained the name Yeshua inscribed within a fish. The fish is an early Judeo-Christian symbol honoring the memory of Jesus. ><

Mariamene e Mara ("Mary, also known as the Master" or possibly "Mary and Martha"). There is some controversy surrounding this inscription. The question is whether this is a reference to Mary Magdalene or sisters Mary and Martha of Bethany. According to the Gnostic Gospels, Mary Magdalene was a leader in the early Christian movement. Her relationship with Jesus was also perceived by the disciples as being closer than theirs was. However, these circumstances would not be enough to bestow her with the title of "Master." If this is Mary Magdalene, necessity requires that she was married to Jesus in order to be interred in the family tomb.

Mary of Bethany was thought to be the matriarch of the family that consisted of herself, sister Martha, and brother Lazarus. Jewish tradition established the eldest sibling as the Master of a parentless household. That Mary and Martha would be placed in the same ossuary is improbable. Therefore, the most likely person whose bones are found in this ossuary is Mary of Bethany. Known to be fond of Jesus, her family's affluence may have allowed her to purchase the tomb. Adding further confusion is that Mary Magdalene and Mary of Bethany are sometimes mentioned as being one and the same individual.

Yoseh (Joseph). This inscription is in dispute as well. It is equally possible that it represents the Joseph mentioned in "Jesus, son of Joseph" or that it could be the name of a brother of Jesus. If it is the name of the "father" of Jesus, then it likely represents a nickname used within the family. The name Yoseh is extremely rare and does not appear at all in the Hebrew Mishnah.

Maria (Mariam or Mary). Mary was a common name in the time of Jesus, as was Mariam. It is not clear whether this would be the mother of Jesus or not, but it is highly likely if this is indeed the family tomb of Jesus. Although first names were all that people typically used, Mary's proper name would be Mariam bat Joakim (Mary, daughter of Joachim).

Yehuda bar Yeshua (Judah, son of Jesus). If this is a son of Jesus, it would point to Jesus being married. Jesus also had a brother named Judah. Opponents of the notion that the Talpiot site is the family tomb of Jesus falsely assert that the name on this ossuary is "Judas." They propose that Jesus would never have given his son that name. However, if Judas the disciple was the alleged betrayer of Jesus, that betrayal would likely have occurred after the birth of Judas, Jesus' son. It is unlikely that Jesus survived the crucifixion. If he fathered a child, it would have been before the cross. Therefore, the Judas argument is spurious.

Yose, the youngest brother of Jesus. (See Matthew 27:56 and Mark 15:47.)

One of the ossuaries disappeared soon after it was cataloged. It did not bear a name inscription. An additional ossuary that was found prior to the discovery of the Talpiot Tomb bore the inscription "James, brother of Jesus." The patina and external surface of this ossuary were tested to determine its chemical/soil composition, as it was thought that this ossuary may have originated at the Talpiot Tomb. Indeed, it tested as being identical to the other ossuaries. It has been proposed that this ossuary may have been located near the entrance to the tomb and was dug out and taken at some point prior to the discovery of the remaining ossuaries. The inclusion of the James ossuary substantially increases the likelihood that this is, in fact, Jesus' family tomb.

There are critics who claim that the Talpiot Tomb could not be the family tomb of Jesus since his family lived in Nazareth, not Jerusalem. However, it is apparent from the scriptures that James, the brother of Jesus, moved to Jerusalem and was a major leader of the Christian movement early on. It is very possible that the entire family moved to Jerusalem after the crucifixion of Jesus. Nazareth at that time remained a small village on a trade route. In addition, Joseph was originally from Bethlehem, and he may well have had family there. While it is reasonably clear that the family of Jesus was poor during his younger years, it is possible that the family's economic circumstances improved during his time of ministry. It is conceivable that an expensive family tomb was within their reach. However, it is more likely that someone like Joseph of Arimathea may have given the family a tomb out of respect for Jesus.

The Talpiot Tomb is located about five kilometers (three miles) south of the old city in east Jerusalem. The original garden tomb of Jesus was located near the hill of Golgotha, where he was crucified. It now lies under the Church of the Holy Sepulchre, which was built by Helena, mother of Constantine, in 330 CE.[1] No one disputes that Jesus did not remain in the tomb that he was originally placed in by Joseph of Arimathea. It would seem logical that his permanent interment might be located away from the old city where it would not be seen. The tomb is not marked with a family name but does bear some symbols on its facade. There has been speculation as to what they represent, but no one knows for sure what they mean.[2]

While there are those who believe that the Talpiot Tomb is the family tomb of Jesus, and that it was indeed his bones found in the ossuary marked with his name, there is currently no way that anyone can be certain. Mitochondrial DNA testing was done to determine if the bone fragments found in the Jesus ossuary were related to the person whose remains were in the Mary Magdalene ossuary. The testing proved that there was no matrilineal relationship between them. Therefore, they could have been husband and wife. The other possibility is that they may have had a paternal connection, making them half-brother and half-sister. If Joseph was their common father, then he must have been married twice and had children by his first wife. Also, if Joseph fathered Jesus, which is contrary to the scriptural record, "Yeshua" would, of necessity, be mortal.[3]

There are additional bone fragments from the Jesus ossuary that may be tested at some point in the future. This testing would be done to establish the relationship of the person in the Jesus bone box to the others in the tomb. There is enormous resistance to testing the remains any further. This resistance purportedly comes from the highest levels of political and religious leadership. Clearly, the impact of establishing that Jesus of Nazareth lies in the ossuary bearing his name would be monumental. It would turn the Christian world upside down. Of course, the Christian community, and others,

---

[1] "Church of the Holy Sepulchre."
[2] Lutgen, "The Talpiot Tomb."
[3] Jacobovici and Pellegrino, "The Jesus Family Tomb."

vehemently reject the notion that this is the tomb of Jesus and that he may have been married and had a son. If Jesus did not rise from the dead and ascend to heaven, then he was a mere mortal and not God incarnate.

***

Commentary

When Simcha Jacobovici released his controversial documentary introducing the Talpiot Tomb to the world, both praise and condemnation rose up in response. Predictably, believers and detractors lined up according to their pre-existing beliefs about Jesus of Nazareth. After reading commentaries opposing the Talpiot Tomb theory, this author found nothing that unequivocally debunked it. As usual, there is an abundance of duplicitous objection based in rationalization and simple dismissal.

It remains inexplicable that Christians are willing to believe a man from the first century resurrected himself from being dead while they summarily dismiss all evidence that challenges that misguided contention. They may then turn and point a critical finger at rational people who find no merit in the Son of God theory— many of whom gave it a genuine try. Were it proven that Jesus of Nazareth's bones were in the Yeshua ossuary, fact-resistant Christians would refuse to believe it— paradoxically just as Jesus' own disciples refused to believe reports that he had risen from the dead.

Was Jesus Married?

Speculation on whether Jesus was married or not is based, in part, on descriptions of his conduct with Mary Magdalene, out of whom Jesus cast seven demons (Luke 8:2 and Mark 16:9). Nowhere in the Bible is it written that Mary Magdalene was, or ever had been, a prostitute, as she has frequently been characterized. John 20 includes a description of Mary Magdalene's encounter with the risen Jesus in the tomb. While standing behind her, Jesus called Mary by name. She turned and realized who it was she had been talking to. She called him "Rabboni," a term used to describe those who are teachers, masters, and spiritual instructors. It is synonymous with the title Rabbi. It is known that Jesus read the Tanakh aloud and taught in the Temple. He frequented synagogues as well, where he preached and taught. In order for a Hebrew man to preach or teach in the Temple, he had to be a rabbi. Although the term did not mean exactly what it does today, Jesus was required to have the approval of the Jewish Temple hierarchy in order to participate as he did—as a rabbi.

Even in the first century, rabbis were required to marry in order to comply with Genesis 1:28, where God commanded Adam and Eve to be fruitful and multiply. Further, it was expected of Jewish men in general to be married and produce children. (Gen. 2:24) In fact, the Jewish Messiah, Mashiach ben David, was prophesied to have at least one son who would rule after he was gone. Accordingly, Jesus would be expected to have a son in order to bolster his claim to being the Messiah. Presenting himself as the Messiah without having a wife or a son would cast doubt over his candidacy for that holy position. Even so, Jewish marriage law would have prevented Jesus from marrying an Israelite woman. As discussed previously, a male born out of wedlock could not enter into marriage with a Jewess, but he could marry a Gentile. There is no possibility that the Jewish Messiah would have a Gentile wife.

Jewish leaders who were members of the Temple institutions—Pharisees, Sadducees, and the Sanhedrin—were required to be married. It is likely, if not certain, that the Apostle Paul had been married at one time, since he had been a member of the Sanhedrin. Wives of the many men noted in the New Testament are almost never mentioned. Those who are had some place in the narrative so that their mention is relevant. It almost seems as if wives and family members are purposely kept secret. No one knows who the apostles were married to, or if they were married at all. In the same way, no one knows who Jesus may have been married to as the Bible does not say, nor does it indicate anywhere that he *was* married.[1] Most New Testament Bible scholars teach that he was being saved for "the Bride of Christ," which is the Church (see Ephesians 5:22–33). Christians believe that Jesus and his bride will be married after he returns. Since the resurrection, the Bride of Christ has been betrothed (promised to, engaged) to Jesus. It has been a long engagement.

All four Gospels mention Mary Magdalene as being at the tomb and that she was part of the group of women who were going to prepare the body of Jesus. Jewish law strictly forbade any female who was not an immediate family member to be involved in touching the body of a deceased man. Only the wives, mothers, and sisters could be present during the preparation. Accordingly, it follows that Mary Magdalene must have been the wife of Jesus; otherwise, she was in violation of Jewish law. Violating Jewish law was a sin, and it was unlikely that sin would be introduced into the scene at the tomb, or if so, recorded in the scripture.

It is thought-provoking to speculate that Mary Magdalene may not have been Jewish after all. Although it is believed she was a Jew, her mannerisms and cultural proclivities were said to be Canaanite. She was born in Magda, which is situated on the northwest shore of the Sea of Galilee. It is a short fifteen miles from the border of Syro-Phoenicia and its ethnic Canaanite population.

---

[1] Kraut, "Was Jesus Married?"

Jesus would have been free to marry her if she was indeed a Gentile.[2] Considering all of this, it is at least a reasonable argument to claim that Jesus *was* married. And if he was, he was most likely married to Mary Magdalene.

---

[2] "Mary Magdalene Biography."

Contrasting the Hebrew Bible and the Christian Old Testament

When questioning an orthodox Jew regarding the interpretation of an "Old Testament" scripture, you might be surprised when a look of consternation is forthcoming. You see, Judaism does not acknowledge the Christian Old Testament, otherwise known as the Old Covenant. When Jesus proclaimed his "New Covenant," he asserted that it abrogated the Laws of the Mosaic Covenant with respect to sin. Jesus insisted that his death on the cross was a final sacrifice that satisfied the Laws of Moses and atoned for the sins of all Jews. His extravagant claim was utterly rejected by Judaism.

Jesus also defiled the Davidic Covenant by attempting to replace David with himself. Judaism rejected this false claim, as well. Jesus never was the Christ to them. A pragmatic observation is that, in the end, the New Covenant simply served to rationalize that Jesus died a heretic because he was not deemed to be the Messiah after proclaiming he was.

Although Christians are pleased to offer that their Old Testament is identical to the Hebrew Bible, that is untrue. For one thing, the Hebrew Bible has been augmented by commentary from within Jewish tradition. This commentary is found in the Talmud and Midrash. Therefore, attempts by other theologies to translate it will deviate from its true and intended content. A paper presented at BecomingJewish.org stated that "The Christian Old Testament contains books and additions that are considered apocryphal by Judaism."[1]

In an article written for the Huffington Post, Dr. Joel Hoffman cites differences in perceptions related to "textual

---

[1] "Tanakh versus Old Testament."

misunderstandings that originate with flawed translation techniques, including the use of erroneous old translations and the misunderstanding of metaphor."[2] Further, the Old Testament and the Hebrew Bible differ in terms of the number of their texts and the order they appear in. There are thirty-nine books in the Christian Old Testament and twenty-four in the Tanakh. Jews claim the ordering of books influences the overall perspective of what is being told.

Scriptural Revision

For the purpose of portraying Jesus as the Christ, a number of key passages were "expropriated" from the Hebrew Bible by New Testament authors. Gospel scribes were audacious in lifting Old Testament scriptures from their proper context before inserting versions of them into the New Testament. Misinterpretation, misapplication, and mistranslation commonly influenced and changed the appropriate meanings of Hebrew Bible texts. Notable appellative changes were also made. The passage found in Isaiah 7:14 is an apropos example. As previously recounted, it relates the story of the virgin and her baby Immanuel.

Immanuel and Isaiah 7:14

The two most relevant verses are:

> Behold, a virgin shall be with child, and shall bring forth a son, and they shall call his name Immanuel, which being interpreted is, God with us (Matt. 1:23).

> Therefore, the Lord Himself will give you a sign: Behold, the virgin shall conceive and bear a Son, and shall call His name Immanuel (Isa. 7:14).

For many believers, it appears superficially plausible for Isaiah 7:14 to be prophetically linked to the birth of Jesus. It is nonetheless a

---

[2] Hoffman, "Five Ways Your Bible Translation Distorts the Original Meaning of the Text."

ruse to do so. The theme of this passage is simple and straightforward. There is no messianic usage that is valid or appropriate. Instead, it represents a near-future promise made to King Ahaz by God through his prophet, Isaiah. That promise was that God would be with King Ahaz in his struggle against invading enemies. God gave Ahaz a sign. That sign was that a child named Immanuel ("God with us") would be born to an *almah*. *Almah* is a Hebrew word for a maiden or young woman of childbearing age. It does not describe whether she is a virgin or not. The Hebrew word for virgin is *betulah*. There is a strong insinuation that the maiden in the promise was not a virgin since the word *betulah* was not used in the Hebrew text. The words of Isaiah 7:14 were then changed and re-scripted by the Greek writers of the Septuagint. They recast the Hebrew word *almah*, changing it to the Greek word *parthenos*, which means "virgin." This created the opportunity for New Testament apologists to falsely assert that this verse is prophetic about Jesus. Taking the deception further, Christian versions of the Old Testament then capitalized the words "Son" and "His." This was done to impart deity to the original noun "son" and the determiner "his." Matthew repeats the error in his Christmas narrative. *Jesus never cited this verse as a prophetic reference about himself.*

The Red Sea Crossing

As noted above, Greek translators of the Hebrew Bible who were responsible for the crafting of the Septuagint often seemed eager to embellish and even change circumstances where it suited them to do so. Many of these mistakes found their way into the New Testament. An example is found in the story of the Red Sea crossing.

The crossing of the Red Sea by the fleeing Jews is an iconic story. Books have been written and movies made, all telling how God parted the Red Sea, thus allowing the trapped Jews to escape their rapidly approaching enemy. The less spectacular version, told by mainstream historians, establishes that the Jews actually crossed a shallow lake known as the Reed Sea. In the third century BCE, the writers of the Septuagint inaccurately translated the original Hebrew, *yam suph*, into the Greek *erythra thalassa*, or Red Sea. The error was never corrected, and it created a significant embellishment to the Exodus story. The Reed Sea, now dried up and gone, was located near the north end of the Gulf of Suez. The crossing of the Red Sea is only a make-believe miracle that qualifies as nothing more than wishful thinking. The Reed Sea was very shallow at the point where the Jews likely crossed. Speculation is that high winds pushed the shallow waters of the Reed Sea enough to create a dry crossing point where a sand bar existed. That the mistake was never corrected seems to point a finger at Greek translators who may well have turned a blind eye to the truth in favor of forwarding an agenda. We have witnessed this illusive behavior before. It remains an issue, however, that the story continues to be told as if it were true, even when scholars and expositors know full well that it is a product of mistranslation and is a significant misrepresentation of the truth.

David and Goliath

In 1 Samuel 17:49–51 is found the well-known tale of David and Goliath. Little David chose five smooth stones from off the ground and with sling in hand, confronted the giant Philistine. David taunted Goliath and then removed a stone from his waist pouch. He placed the stone in his sling and hurled it at the giant. Goliath fell to the ground, dead. The next verse tells that David prevailed over the mighty Philistine warrior and had killed him with a sling and a stone. However, the verse that follows (v. 51) states that David ran to the fallen body of the giant, drew his sword, and "killed him" by cutting off his head. Therefore, in back-to-back verses, David killed Goliath twice using different weapons. Alas, the duplicity does not end there.

In 2 Samuel 21:19–20 is a repeat story of the death of Goliath, only this time it was Elhanan, son of Jaare-Oregim, who killed the giant Philistine. The original manuscripts contain this, but it was changed in later translations. For instance, the King James translation of 1611 carries an addition which places the words "brother of" in front of "Goliath" (v. 19). "The brother of" is written in italics, indicating it was added by writers who translated it from earlier versions. There was a need to promote David as a great warrior, and so he was later bestowed with the credit of killing the Philistine, instead of Elhanan.

Of interest is the revelation that Goliath may not have been a giant at all. Dead Sea scrolls found in Qumran contain manuscripts indicating that Goliath was "four cubits and a span" in height and not six cubits and a span as reported in the Christian Old Testament. Four cubits and a span converts to six feet, six inches, which is much shorter than the nine feet, six inches stated in later texts that appear to have been embellished. A report by Josephus the Jewish historian corroborates the new finding.

No expositor of the Bible is suggesting that a deception is buried here that needs to be corrected. Such things are left "as is" for fear of casting any doubt on the veracity of God's word.

Paul's Deception

Sophistic behavior was not exclusive to the writers of the Septuagint. Purposefully mendacious interpretation errors, sometimes dubbed *textual hijacking,* are common throughout the New Testament. An example is found in Galatians 3:16, where we find the Apostle Paul re-inventing a passage from Genesis. He writes: "Now to Abraham and his seed were the promises made. He saith not, And to seeds, as of many; but as of one, And to thy seed, which is Christ" (Gen. 13:15–16).

Paul is either lacking in his understanding of Hebrew, which is unlikely, or he is boldly reworking this Hebrew text. Although "seed" used in Genesis 13 is singular in form, it clearly is plural in meaning. The Hebrew language does not contain a plural form of seed. In the Genesis passage, God said: "For all the land which thou seest, to thee will I give it, and to thy seed forever. And I will make thy seed as the dust of the earth; so that if a man can number the dust of the earth, then shall thy seed also be numbered."

If Abraham's seed will be multiplied to number beyond "the dust of the earth," it obviously carries a strictly plural connotation. Paul has tried to put Christ into this promise, but it is a clear and intentional distortion of the original meaning to do so.

In a sense, the practice of textual hijacking makes a mockery of the term "inspired scripture," especially when it comes to the New

Testament. If God's words are true and inspired, they should not be open to re-invention. That this has been done explains why the truth of the Bible, especially as it relates to the Godhood of Jesus, is often difficult to ascertain and then believe.

The Physical Jesus

In 1940, American artist Warner Sallman painted a portrait known as the *Head of Christ*. It has become the most iconic visage of Jesus in the world today. Sallman's painting has been lithographically reproduced over 500 million times. When individuals from around the world are asked to describe what their mind's eye envisions when thinking of Jesus Christ, the number-one response is Sallman's *Head of Christ* painting. The portrait hangs in almost every Christian church in the United States. It has been said that this painting transformed Jesus into a worldwide celebrity. The *Head of Christ* is even more popular than Leonardo da Vinci's *The Last Supper*.[1]

Sallman once stated that the *Head of Christ* image came to him in a dream in 1924. Incredibly, a number of miracles have been attributed to the painting. The primary sources for the reports come from the Coptic Orthodox Church. They mostly describe miraculous healings, but also include reports that criminal conduct has been interrupted when thieves cast their eyes toward the painting.

The oldest known image of Jesus was discovered in Syria. It dates to about 235 CE. He is depicted as being a beardless young man of dignified demeanor. His hair is close-cropped, and he is wearing a tunic. It is not known who painted the image or whether it represents an accurate depiction based on written reports from the time of Jesus.[2] A 2015 *Popular Mechanics* article asserted that Jesus "is often depicted as being much taller than his disciples, lean, with long flowing hair, fair skin and light-colored eyes. Familiar though this image may be, it is inherently flawed. A person with these

---

[1] "Head of Christ."
[2] "Depiction of Jesus."

features and physical presence would have looked very different from everyone else in the region where Jesus lived and ministered."[3]

From analysis of first-century skeletal remains, anthropologists and archeologists have been able to determine that the average Galilean adult male during the time of Jesus was 5'1" to 5'4" tall. A weight associated with that height would fall within a range of 110 to 120 pounds. Short hair was the cultural style of that day. Some have claimed Jesus had long hair based on an assumption that he was a Nazarite. However, it is never mentioned in the Bible that Jesus took a Nazarite vow. The Apostle Paul, who was not a contemporary of Jesus per se, nevertheless may have seen him at Passover in Jerusalem during the years prior to his conversion. In 1 Corinthians 11:14, Paul argues that it is a "dishonor" for a man to have long hair. Since he may have seen Jesus, or at least knew of his appearance, it is doubtful that he would say such a thing if he was aware that Jesus wore long hair.

In 1998, British and Israeli scientists, including a forensic anthropologist, a medical illustrator, and a forensic sculptor, undertook to create an accurate picture of Jesus, based on evidence.[4] Three male skulls from the Galilee region, all dating from the time of Jesus, were subjected to various diagnostic tests. Computerized axial tomography (CAT) scans were used to create three-dimensional images that proved to be valuable in the examination of the skulls for details that could contribute to their analysis. Certain features stood out as being intrinsic to these particular skulls. For instance, the width of the skulls in the parietal region was greater than that of skulls from other regions and ethnicities of that time. The end result was an image that is dramatically different than the Sallman painting or the look of Jim Caviezel (as Jesus) in the movie *The Passion of the Christ*. Nevertheless, many Christians who have seen images of the scientifically derived Jesus are appalled and even angered. Once published, the image of Jesus created by Warren Sallman became fixed in the minds of believers as being "what Jesus really looked like." How unfortunate that deception prevails and, predictably, the truth is subordinated to what those who follow Jesus

---

[3] Neuendorf, "Medical Artist Reveals What Jesus Christ Looked Like."
[4] Taylor, "What Did Jesus Really Look Like?"

want to believe. It would be interesting to see what effect an actual picture of Jesus would have on believers. There is a phenomenon known as "the tyranny of looks." It often plays a role in the success of people who are attractive.[5] Most notably, the prevailing vision of Jesus has surely contributed to, or at least enhanced, the modern world's proclivity to be drawn to him.

---

[5] Maestripieri, "The Truth About Why Beautiful People are More Successful."

The Son of Aten and the Many Sons of Gods

The contention that the holy family was in Egypt for a given period of time lays the groundwork for an interesting parallel between the life and ministry of Jesus and the reign of the Egyptian Pharaoh Akhenaten. Also known as Amenhotep IV, he ruled over Egypt from 1352 to 1336 BCE.

All Egyptian pharaohs believed they were deities. They presided over a religious system that was widely polytheistic. Temples abounded and priests interceded on behalf of a multitude of gods. Akhenaten means "Living Spirit of God." A rebellious radical, he turned the entire structure of Egyptian polytheism on its head. Early in his reign, he issued a decree that all gods were banned except for the sun disk god, Aten. He instituted monotheism in the form of Atenism, closed many temples, and moved the religious center of Egypt at Thebes to a new site 250 miles north. There, at El-Amarna, he built lavish new temples for the worship of Aten.[1]

Central to the Jesus comparison is Akhenaten's declaration that he was the Son of Aten and only he could intercede on behalf of his people. Of course, this caused a major backlash within the religious community of Egypt. When Akhenaten died, the Son of Aten and his wife, Nefertiti, were erased from Egyptian history, as they had come to be despised. In much the same manner, Jesus was seen as a rebel who attempted to change the Hebrew religious order in Jerusalem. He believed himself to be the Son of God and "God made flesh." His assertion that only he was "the way, the truth and the life" offended and threatened the religious establishment of the day. Ultimately, they rid themselves of him in order to maintain longstanding Jewish tradition.

---

[1] "Akhenaten (Amenhotep IV) the Heretic Pharoah"

Another renowned ruler, somewhat more contemporary to Jesus, was Alexander the Great. He ruled as a pharaoh of Egypt during the early Ptolemaic period (336 BCE to 323 BCE.). In addition to his claim of being the Son of Zeus, the Greek supreme god, Alexander the Great declared himself to also be the Son of Amun, the King of the Egyptian gods.

There are fifty-three demigods in Greek mythology who were said to be half god and half man. Many were the product of a Greek god taking a mortal wife. All of the demigods possessed supernatural strength and powers. A strong Greek cultural and religious influence remained at the time of Jesus. Demigods were "gods made man." So it was that Jesus claimed to be "God made flesh."

It is not known if Jesus ever drew inspiration from Alexander the Great, Akhenaten, or anyone else, but there are such strong parallels and cultural inferences that it seems at least plausible that he did. Since it was a common practice for rulers to declare themselves gods or sons of gods, it would be reasonable for someone claiming to be the Jewish Messiah to also proclaim that he was the Son of God.

Belief

I do not mean by this declaration to condemn those who believe otherwise; they have the same right to their belief that I have to mine. But it is necessary to the happiness of man, that he be mentally faithful to himself. Infidelity does not consist in believing, or disbelieving; it consists in professing to believe what he does not believe.
—Thomas Paine

Humankind has always believed in and worshipped gods. Hardly a culture, tribe or civilization has existed that did not seek out the favor and protection of one or more of them. Belief in God has served to give rationality to the human experience and has helped to explain the unexplained. God gives those who believe a place to take their petitions and prayers. In trusting God to intervene on their behalf, an imagined sense of control is achieved when circumstances may otherwise seem hopeless. For many, belief in God may help answer the basic questions of their existence: Why are we here? Where did we come from?

Religions owe their very existence to belief. An appeal that is commonly voiced to religious adherents implores them to "just believe." Religious expositors may go so far as to teach that belief in God is an innate requirement of the human experience. They propose that we are programmed to seek out and need God. Once found, they say, a connection with God is then accomplished through belief coupled with unwavering faith.

Belief, Emotions, and Mental Health

Belief in an all-caring higher power often plays an important role in the arena of human emotions. Belief in Jesus may offer a sense of security to those who are insecure. It can give relief, in the form of forgiveness, to those who are riddled with guilt. It purportedly offers eternal life to those who fear death, as well as protection for those who fear the world they live in. Trusting Jesus may even provide love to those who feel unloved. Nearly all the emotional needs that humans experience can potentially be met through the simple act of belief. With beliefs, it is sometimes possible for followers to invent solutions to the problems that plague them. And although those solutions may be based on some degree of contrivance, they often appear to work for those who believe they will.

In an article written for Psychology Today, psychiatrist Abigail Brenner states, "Recent research has shown that you are what you believe. Your perception of reality is determined by the beliefs you hold. This does not necessarily make them real, except for the fact that you believe they are."[1] Dr. Brenner's comments strike a common chord with a proverb spoken many hundreds of years ago by the spiritual practitioner Gautama Siddhartha Buddha. Drawing upon his prodigious wisdom, Buddha taught that; "We become what we believe. All that we are arises with our thoughts. With our thoughts, we make our world."[2] If reality is a reflection of one's strongest beliefs, it must follow that changing your beliefs carries the potential to change your reality. This truism applies when individuals convert to religious institutions and then adopt their new and discrete ways of thinking.

There is sometimes a fine line between belief and mental illness. In terms of behaviors, they seem to share a handful of common characteristics. What is it that separates the two?

Typically, the concept of belief begins as a matter of the will. People chose to believe. Mental illness, on the other hand, is generally something that afflicts an individual. No one desires to become mentally unwell. But if the origins of belief are initially willful, how might it be characterized after becoming more deeply ingrained?

There is a point where a belief system becomes an integral part of the entire mindset—where it becomes a key element in the individual's worldview—part of their "personhood." Religious ideology can potentially infest every aspect of a believer's life. Devout belief may come to have a controlling influence over the

---

[1] Brenner, "You Are What You Believe."
[2] Kynaston, "The Mind is Everything."

way religious adherents think. Many Christians believe the arrogant notion that they enjoy a superior perspective based in divine enlightenment. They have been taught that "normal" (rational) thinking is often faulty and should not be trusted, especially where it conflicts with biblical teachings. As such, it may represent a subtle presentation of thought reform.

Thought reform is facilitated by the subordination of the will to think for oneself. Cognitive thought reform is a primary tool used in brainwashing. It is also an unwitting strategy employed by Christianity. The Apostle Paul identified this type of thought reform. He described the process as, "the putting off of the old self, and the putting on of the new" (Ephesians 4:22–24). Paul also beseeched believers: "not to be conformed to this world: but be transformed by the *renewing of your minds*." (Romans 12:1–3). The dynamic of this so-called renewing process is primarily a matter of forcing cognitive changes. Doing so facilitates a new way of seeing things.
In 1 Cor. 2:14, Paul writes:

> But the natural man does not receive the things of the Spirit of God, for they are foolishness to him; neither can he know them, because they are only discerned spiritually.

From a secular perspective, it is Bible believers who are seeing truth in spiritual vacuousness. As the above verse notes, their thinking seems foolish to the "natural man." Paul's argument needs to be re-directed. It more properly applies to those who have foregone rational thinking and re-assigned their thoughts to coincide with the dictates of biblical dogma. In this context, godly people see what their faith instructs them to see. They see what their spiritual bias implores them to see. Thus, they have an obstructed view of reality.

Cognitive distortion is a term coined to explain how irrational thoughts can influence one's emotions. Everyone experiences cognitive distortions to some degree and not all of them lead to negative behaviors. However, in their more extreme forms cognitive distortions may be harmful[3]. If there is a religious

---

[3] Staff, et al. "Cognitive Distortions."

circumstance that can promote harmful cognitive distortions, it would likely be represented by the same factors that contribute to Religious Trauma Syndrome.

Religious Trauma Syndrome

Religious Trauma Syndrome (RTS) is a complex type of Post-Traumatic Stress Disorder (PTSD) that is associated with the chronic abuses of authoritarian, restrictive and controlling religions. Those that demand or require an unwavering and zealous commitment are especially implicated. *The same symptomology may also be present with those who decide to break away from their faith.* The primary symptoms expressed in RTS include anxiety, depression, insomnia, and nightmares. These individuals often feel intense guilt and confusion. Many engage in substance abuse as a way to cope with their symptoms.[4]

Unfortunately, this syndrome is somewhat new to psychology and there may be a shortage of mental health professionals who are trained to treat it. RTS has undoubtedly been around since the advent of religion. In the modern era of mental health treatment, it has been recognized by a variety of different but related diagnostic nomenclatures.

Many RTS sufferers have come forward with their stories—the pain and suffering that comes with RTS can be crippling. As just mentioned, the loss of one's belief system carries the potential to create as much chaos as was present *before* the individual parted from their faith. It is wise to seek help from a qualified mental health professional once the symptoms of RTS are identified in anyone who is suffering. You may feel as though it is imperative to *get out* of your religious circumstances but seek help when you do. It is not always as simple as walking away from church on Sunday.

Cognitive Dissonance

Cognitive dissonance is a chronic emotional condition wherein the sufferer is perplexed due to an inability to reconcile conflicting

---

[4] Winell. "Religious Trauma Syndrome."

beliefs. The beliefs are typically of a religious, political, or moral nature. James, the brother of Jesus, may have understood the nature of cognitive dissonance—at least as it applies to doubt and uncertainty.

> For he who doubts is like a wave of the sea, driven and tossed by the wind. For let not that man suppose that he will receive anything from the Lord; [for] he is a double-minded man, unstable in all his ways (James 1:6–8).

Unfortunately, faith and reality are often at odds. They may represent two different, and often conflicting, frames of reference. For an individual who is deeply sincere about both, a psychological tug of war may result. The ensuing cognitive dissonance may ultimately become deeply distressing.

An example is represented by a believer's reluctance or inability to embrace biblical content that conflicts with scientific and historical facts. A devout believer may be intensely dependent on his or her faith, while concurrently being a critical thinker who is educated in the sciences. Compartmentalizing may work for some, but others find it to be ineffective and disingenuous. Worse yet is the tendency to disregard the conflict or to fail to recognize it altogether. If the conflict is not resolved, depression, anxiety and resentment may eventuate. Chronic long-term mental conflict, and/or bitterness, may even contribute to physical illness.[5]

Philosophy and Beliefs

Epistemology is a branch of philosophy concerned with belief and its interaction with the theory of knowledge. Epistemology also explores other concepts related to belief. For instance, it investigates how belief is distinguished from simple opinion.

Fideism (Latin, faithism) is a branch of epistemology which asserts that true knowledge depends on faith. It goes so far as to declare that faith and reason often oppose each other. Fideistic methodology attempts to protect faith via intellectual insulation. In

---

[5] Merkes. "Bitterness Makes the Heart Grow Sicker."

his book *Christian Apologetics: A Comprehensive Case for Biblical Faith*, Professor Douglas Groothuis, asserts that fideism essentially tries to; "make belief a self-certifying and self-enclosed reality that needs no intellectual fortification." He further relates: "Fideists believe that because faith is a divine gift that serves as a channel or means through which one approaches and understands God, human reasoning cannot establish the validity of any religion."[6] Groothuis considers that classical apologetics builds its cases from the ground up, while fideism excuses itself from even attempting to construct a coherent defense of belief. Some might consider that approach on a par with simple avoidance.

To be sure, there are defenders of theology who feel that fideism goes a long way in discrediting believers and belief. Followers of "natural theology" hold to traditional arguments for the existence of God that are based in rationality. These non-fideists assert that blind faith is not true faith and that belief in God should be able to stand up to scrutiny during debate.

Scientific Investigation

Scientific studies are beginning to explore the many facets of belief. Scientists have proposed that the fear of death, combined with normal mental processes, predispose us to believe in God—but there is little objective evidence that we are hardwired to do so.

New research, sponsored and overseen by the University of Oxford, reveals that humans seem to have natural tendencies to believe in gods and an afterlife. These worldwide studies suggest that people from diverse cultural settings instinctively believe that some part of their mind, soul or spirit lives on after death. The research, which was primarily empirical and analytical in nature, concluded that "humans are predisposed to believe in gods and an afterlife", and that "theology is a reasoned response to what is a basic 'impulse' of the human mind." Of some intrigue is the finding that attempts to suppress religion are likely to be short-lived, as "human thought seems to be rooted to religious concepts, such as

---

[6] Groothuius. "On Fidiesm"

the existence of supernatural agents or gods, and the possibility of an afterlife or pre-life."[7]

Shaheen Lakhan, associate professor of neurology and medical education at California University of Science and Medicine, recently reported; "The neuroscientific study of religious and spiritual phenomena remains in its infancy. There is mounting evidence of a biological correlate to these phenomena; however, this does not necessarily negate an actual spiritual component." According to Dr. Lakhan, there is little known and much to be learned with regard to the biological nature and origins of belief.[8] Biological anthropologist Greg Laden contributed on ScienceBlogs.com his feeling that; "religiosity—a personal belief in god, spirits, the supernatural, etc.—would emerge in human societies on its own if it was not there already." He went on to say; "However, it is not the inevitable outcome of typical development, as coded for by genes."[9]

Why is it that some people are more willing than others to believe in God? An article from Scientific American (*How Critical Thinkers Lose Faith in God*, 2012) reports how "religious belief drops when analytical thinking rises." New research suggests that the inclination to believe in God bears a significant correlation with the degree to which people are intuitive. The article also reports on previous research that found "people differ in their tendency to see intentions and causes in the world."[10] It is more likely for intuitive thinkers to see God's will being revealed in the events and circumstances of their lives. This tendency may possibly be related to the phenomenon known as *apophenia*. Those who are prone to apophenia see patterns and meaning in unrelated events. Meanwhile, analytical thinkers tend to be more skeptical. The view they hold of their world is more straightforward. They are not prone to believe that unseen forces (e.g., God) are at work in directing their futures.

---

[7] University of Oxford. "Humans 'Predisposed' to Believe in Gods and the Afterlife."

[8] Lakhan. "The God Brain."

[9] Laden. "Why I Would Believe in God if I Wasn't an Athiest."

[10] Grenwal. "How Critical Thinkers Lose Their Faith in God."

In 2016, the University of Southern California (USC) Brain and Creativity Institute, in cooperation with the USC Social Behavior Lab, conducted studies aimed at evaluating beliefs. The goal was to understand the dynamics of what drives the psychology behind tightly held core beliefs. Participants in the study underwent magnetic resonance imaging (MRI), the goal being to target and assess brain changes during periods of *belief attacks*. The study concluded that the part of the brain that responds to physical threats (the amygdala, or emotional center) also responds to intellectual threats. In other words, it delivers the same fright reaction to threatening information as it does to the threat of a predator or other physical danger.[11]

Core beliefs are those convictions that people hold most deeply. As mentioned, they often develop from childhood and are compounded by life experiences. Core beliefs tend to be rigid and inflexible. They are most often associated with political, spiritual, and moral concepts. These kinds of beliefs are profoundly sensitive to being challenged. To maintain and protect a stable world construct, our brains reject any notion that challenges our core beliefs. When it is revealed that a core belief has been founded on false information, the impact on our emotional self can be devastating.[12]

Patternicity and Conditioning

When it comes to the concept of belief, modern cultures have traditionally, and somewhat unwittingly, participated in conditioning their children to accept the idea of the supernatural. At the most critical time of brain and personality development, children are exposed to mythical characters who are presented as being real. In addition to other mythical and supernatural beings, they are led to believe that there is a Santa Claus and a Tooth Fairy. Accordingly, they are imprinted with the information that belief is appropriate. Although children are not easily fooled, adults sometimes seem

---

[11] Kaplan. "Neural Correlates of Maintaining One's Beliefs in the Face of Counterevidence."

[12] University of Southern California. "Hard-wired. The Brain's Circuitry for Political Belief."

inadvertently intent on overriding their intrinsic sense of caution. To some extent, then, young children may learn to drop their guard against things that would otherwise generate suspicion or distrust. Whether this is harmful is a matter of debate.[13] Fictional material in the form of stories is not considered inappropriate. In fact, it may encourage the development of imagination and creativity. In general, children are not discouraged from believing in fantasy, nor are they taught that it is wrong. The overall impression is that a child's belief in some measure of fantasy is considered quite normal. Whether such belief is genetically encoded has yet to be determined. It *has* been determined, however, that patterns developed from early life experiences may generate *rudimentary* beliefs that often persist into adulthood. They may then be expanded upon in the form of religious belief systems.[14] In other words, we build belief constructs from learned patterns that are established early in life. Future beliefs owe a great deal to the social, emotional, and spiritual experiences of the formative years.

Divided We Fall

The downside to belief is the way it divides us as people. Although there are many reasons why humans engage in war, one of the primary motivations is hatred of those whose religious beliefs differ from our own. Conflict between groups with divergent beliefs has historically brought violence to the forefront. The Crusades were fought because of a clash between two religions and their different beliefs. Islam, a participant in the Crusades, continues to fight amongst itself as factions who disagree seek to control Muslim adherents and enforce their beliefs wherever possible. The Spanish Inquisition was established to expose those who did not believe in, or follow, Church dogma. Thousands were tortured and killed over beliefs. Even now, on any given day there is at least one religious war being fought somewhere in the World. The incongruity lies with the fact that violent behavior is often in direct violation of the very

---

[13] Johnson. "The Santa Clause Debate."
[14] Shermer. "Paternicity."

tenets that are held sacred. But it is not just wars that destroy our peace and force us apart. We humans fight amongst ourselves in ways that are common to everyday life, as well. Religious bias and bigotry have infected nearly every aspect of our modern existence. Differences in beliefs can cause neighbors to ignore neighbors, and family members to shun their own. It is not unusual to sit in a church on Sunday morning and hear the pastor preach how the church across the street is wrong with respect to everything it teaches about God and the Bible. Beliefs are divisive and everyone knows how ugly such situations can get.

An outgrowth of interdenominational disputes is the theological modality known as *apologetics*. Apologetics is the systematic defense of one religious belief against another. It is a war of words where egos clash and angry disagreements play out on paper and in various media venues. Almost always, infighting among Christians is based on differences of scriptural exegesis and areas of doctrinal emphasis. In the end, apologetics is not unifying. It only serves to widen the gap between groups with divergent beliefs.

Ecumenical movements, both domestic and international, have occasionally appeared in an attempt to bring various religious groups together. These groups place peace and unity as their highest priority. However, even when the intent is to look past beliefs toward peaceful coexistence, they have enjoyed limited success. A movement arose in the 1990s to bring Christian men of different denominations together for the greater good of reflecting a favorable picture of Jesus Christ to the world. This group, known as Promise Keepers, sought to challenge godly men to serve as positive examples to their families and communities. Across the country, Promise Keepers filled the largest athletic stadiums to praise God and to spread encouragement. This author, in fact, attended one of these rallies. Following the event, the leader of our group addressed the men I attended with. His take on this attempt at Christian harmony was completely unexpected. It seems he was dismayed that "men of our denomination should be expected to go over and put our arms around guys who don't "believe" like we do." In fairness, this attitude was not typical. Nevertheless, Promise Keepers, as do many ecumenical movements, faded in scope while denominational barriers remained firmly in place.

***

Commentary

There are those who propose that faith and religious belief are good things. Others argue in the opposite direction. The chasm between the two positions seems to lie primarily, amongst other contributing factors, with individual needs for security, meaning and future fate. Not all doubters would run from faith if it were based on believable concepts—or at least ideas that do not conflict with reality. I cannot look past science and history to an irrational belief that conflicts with them. Nor can I dismiss my own experiences and the way their influence has contributed to and molded my faith.

What is also perplexing is the proclivity of religious partisans to sometimes declare they are willing to die for what they believe. Although looked upon as being quite honorable, such talk beckons us to question what it is that brings about this kind of zealous moxie? It is difficult to accept that anyone would surrender their very existence for the purpose of defending deeply held, but objectively unreliable religious beliefs. Inflated egos and pride may be fueling this phenomenon. It stands to reason that if threats to core beliefs produce adrenalin-driven reactions, we are dealing with something that is profound, but in a way that appears to be detrimental. For that reason, it seems incendiary. Certainly, "taking a stand" is a charged phrase. One that can only lead to open disagreement and volatile arguments. In this context, religious beliefs often breed animosity and hatred. How ironic.

After exploring ideas that I could conceivably place belief in, the conclusion reached is that experience, observation and investigated fact must participate as primary elements in my belief system. Because I am very analytical and have a skeptical eye, I now measure potential beliefs against what I know to be unequivocal truth. The level of certainty necessary for me to adopt a strong conviction or idea is quite high. Though not required, verification is most certainly desirable. And lastly, there is no room whatsoever for an irrational belief that creates conflict with factual truth.

Students of philosophy might hang the label *scientific realist,* or perhaps simply *rationalist,* around my neck, while proponents of religion would consider me a doubting Thomas. It follows that I am a champion of observation and reason. Still, it has become a curiosity to me as to why I am so analytical in the first place? After all, I am not a Vulcan.

Regardless, I have found that maintaining an open and flexible mind leaves me free to learn from life. Having dispatched my faith, I am no longer constricted by tightly held religious dogma or anything else that may be dubious. My curiosity, once constrained by the blinders of fear and guilt, has been released to explore the world ad libitum.

Closing Thoughts

Question with boldness even the existence of a god; because if there be one, he must more approve the homage of reason, than that of blindfolded fear.

—Thomas Jefferson

The Christian life is not an easy one. Great promises are on the menu but, truth be known, promises are just words. Clichéd promises often wear thin over time. Many believers "fight the good fight," only to finish weary and disappointed. At road's end, despite their best efforts, many come to realize how patently unfair life can be. Where spiritual expectations were not met, some question if their decision to become a Christian was the right one. A few cynics query why they ever took up their cross and followed Jesus in the first place. Consider this:

The plan of salvation begins with blind faith. Jesus referred to it as believing without seeing. He called it child-like faith. Perhaps in a vulnerable moment you made a commitment without due consideration. Blind faith is quick and easy. It draws one in without a need for caution. The context is often desperation. Someone said, "Just believe," so you did. Sightless faith champions the meritless acceptance of unevidenced biblical dogma. It boldly positions belief above reason and offers false hope when harsh circumstances become overwhelming. In the realm of Christianity, it becomes the crutch that followers lean on. In fact, without the foundational element of blind faith, many religions would cease to exist.

Belief that is heedless forces rationalizations, excuses, and denials to the center of the Christian walk. They are the defensive tactics believers employ to protect against the failures of their faith. For instance, when bad things beset faithful Christians, unevidenced belief persuades them that God's wrath should not be the implicated causality. Instead, it cunningly submits that he was merely trying to teach something. Not that? Then perhaps the unfortunate circumstance was intended to build character. That is one way to see it when nothing else makes sense. It is apparent that blind faith evokes a perceived need to second-guess every adverse situation. Astute followers may ask if God's motives can ever be established in these instances. Obviously, they cannot be. Instead, blind faith compels confused believers to toss reason to the wind and bury their heads in the sands of mindless trust.

Even more difficult to grasp are those times when fervent prayers for physical healing go unanswered. Your best friend may have contracted cancer, or perhaps your spouse is suddenly near death from a heart condition. Any number of tragic events may transpire wherein Christians must graciously accept that God has a reason for their loved one's afflictions. Prayers may bring a feeling of hope. But in many cases, when prayers go unanswered, hope feels distant. Hence, faithful believers have been taught they are never to question God's intentions for allowing tragedy into their lives. Instead, such things must be considered God's providential will.

Most devout Christians understand that God is unyielding in requiring them to be long-suffering. When scriptural promises seem irreconcilable with today's untoward events, he reminds them that all things are foreordained to demonstrate clarity and meaning in the fullness of time. Those who mindlessly trust Jesus are compelled to believe that today's senseless life circumstances will one day be understood as being part of God's grand plan. Here, blind faith paves the potholes of doubt and confusion with "just wait and you will see."

These types of simplistic explanations are firmly based in rationalization. They do not originate from the insightful or intuitive observations of personal experience. They are not rational or reasonable. Their purpose is to create an illusion that the Christian life makes sense. Many find this process tiring. For some, it leads to disappointment and resentment. In trying times, dispirited believers are left to ask: "Why did this happen to me?" or "Where was God when I needed him?"

Reviewing the life of Jesus from a more critical perspective has made it clear that not all is as it seems. Hopefully, the trail of biblical prevarication uncovered in *Rethinking Jesus* has opened the eyes and minds of troubled Christians—especially those whose faith has been strained to the breaking point. In addition to the evidence presented, it is important to add your own experiences to the mix. Then ask yourself if Christianity is truly working for you. There are two conditions that must be met if you elect to continue your walk with Jesus. The first is your readiness to ignore the many times his promises have rung untrue. The second is your willingness to "just believe."

It is your life to live. Please do not turn it over to something that wants to weaken and control you. Never surrender to irrational notions that will take away your logical perspective. Instead, have faith in yourself. Live according to your own convictions. Remember to remain self-reliant and to always stay strong.

—Dennis Blue

Bibliography

Amirault, Gary. "The Christ Child and the Wise Men." Tentmaker. December 25, 1998. tentmaker.org/articles/ChristChildandWiseMen.html.

Ancient Egypt Online. "Akhenaten | the Heretic Pharaoh." Accessed February 5, 2021. https://www.ancient-egypt-online.com/akhenaten.html.

Barton, William D.D. "The Samaritan Messiah." *The Open Court Magazine,* Vol. XXI, 1907.

Becoming Jewish. "Tanakh Versus Old Testament." Accessed May 11, 2021. becomingjewish.org>tanakh_versus_old_testament.pdf.

Behar, D.M., and Michael F. Hammer. "Extended Y Chromosome Haplotypes Resolve Multiple and Unique Lineages of the Jewish Priesthood." National Library of Medicine. August 8, 2009. https://pubmed.ncbi.nlm.nih.gov/19669163/.

Being Jewish. "What the Messiah is Supposed to Do." Accessed April 28, 2021. beingjewish.com/toshuv/real_messiah.html

Bible Hub. "Strong's Greek: 3860—paradidómi." Accessed March 8, 2021. https://biblehub.com/greek/3860.htm

Biblical Archaeology Society. "Bible Scholar Brent Landau Asks 'who Were the Magi?'." Accessed March 6, 2021. www.biblicalarchaeology.org/daily/people-cultures-in-the-bible/jesus-historical-jesus/bible-scholar-brent-landau-asks-who-were-the-magi/.

Biblioteca Pleyades. "The Lost Gospel of Judas—from the Codex Tchacos." Accessed April 23, 2021. www.bibliotecapleyades.net/mistic/gospel_judas.htm.

Biography. "Mary Magdalene." Last modified June 6, 2021. https://www.biography.com/religious-figure/mary-magdalene#:~:text=One%20of%20Jesus'%20most%20celebrated,her%20birth%20town%20of%20Magdala.

Brown, Michael L. "What Language Did Jesus and the Apostles Speak?" Ask Dr. Brown. January 19, 2013. https://askdrbrown.org/library/what-language-did-jesus-and-apostles-speak.

Brenner, Abigail, M.D. "You Are What You Believe" Psychology Today. 28 November 2012. Accessed 04 Feb. 2021. www.psychologytoday.com/us/blog/in-flux/201211/you-are-what-you-believe.

Covenant Companion. "'Head of Christ' Has Influenced Culture's Image of Jesus for 75 Years." October 29, 2015. https://covenantcompanion.com/2015/10/29/head-of-christ-has-influenced-cultures-image-of-jesus-for-75-years/.

Diocese of Westminster. "44 Prophecies Jesus Christ Fulfilled." Accessed April 11, 2021. https://parish.rcdow.org.uk/swisscottage/wp-content/uploads/sites/52/2014/11/44-Prophecies-Jesus-Christ-Fulfilled.pdf.

Ehrman, Bart. "Jesus and the Hidden Contradictions of the Gospels." NPR. March 12, 2010. npr.org/templates/story/story.php?storyId=124572693.

Evans, Craig A. *The Historical Jesus—Volume 4*. Taylor & Francis, 2004.

Fredriksen, Paula. "When Jesus Celebrated Passover." Wall Street Journal. April 10, 2019. https://www.wsj.com/articles/when-jesus-celebrated-passover-11555685683.

Frenkel, Sheera. "Dig Finds Evidence of Another Bethlehem." National Public Radio. December 25, 2012. https://www.npr.org/2012/12/25/168010065/dig-finds-evidence-of-pre-jesus-bethlehem#:~:text=Dig%20Finds%20Evidence%20Of%20Another%20Bethlehem%20Archaeologists%20are%20unearthing%20evidence,in%20the%20Galilee%20near%20Nazareth.

Fructenbaum, Arnold. "The Messianic Timetable According to Daniel the Prophet." Jews for Jesus. April 20, 2018. jewsforjesus.org/publications/issues/issues-v05-n01/the-messianic-time-table-according-to-daniel-the-prophet.

Funk, Robert W. "Excerpts from the Introduction of the Acts of Jesus." Westar Institute. Accessed February 22, 2021. https://www.westarinstitute.org/projects/the-jesus-seminar/jesus-seminar-phase-2-deeds-of-jesus/excerpt-from-the-introduction-of-the-acts-of-jesus-the-search-for-the-authentic-deeds/.

Funk, Robert W. "The Jesus Seminar Phase 2: The Deeds of Jesus'." Westar Institute. Accessed February 22, 2021. https://www.westarinstitute.org/projects/the-jesus-seminar/jesus-seminar-phase-2-deeds-of-jesus/.

Gallagher, Richard. "As a psychiatrist, I diagnose mental illness. Also, I help spot demonic possession." *The Washington Post*, July 1, 2016. https://www.washingtonpost.com/posteverything/wp/2016/07/01/as-a-psychiatrist-i-diagnose-mental-illness-and-sometimes-demonic-possession/.

Grewal, Daisy, Ph.D. "How Critical Thinkers Lose Their Faith in God." Scientific American. Published by Scientific American, a division of Nature American, Inc. 01 July 2012.

Groothuius, Douglas, Ph.D. "On Fideism" Austin's Blog. 17 June 2012. www.austind.wordpress.com/2012/06/17/on-fideism/ Accessed 27 June 2021.

Helwig-Larsen, Robin. "Jesus, Son of Pantera." The Gospel According to the Romans. November 6, 2011. https://robinhl.com/2011/11/06/jesus-son-of-pantera/.

Hoffman, Joel M. "Five Ways Your Bible Translation Distorts the Original Meaning of the Text." The Huffington Post. October 14, 2011. https://www.huffpost.com/entry/five-ways-your-bible-tran_b_1007058#:~:text=So%20your%20Bible%20translation%20contains,must%20involve%20cancer%20(metaphor)

Ice, Thomas. "Why a Gap in Daniel's 70 Weeks." Bible Prophecy Blog. April 24, 2012. https://www.bibleprophecyblog.com/2012/04/why-gap-in-daniels-70-weeks.html.

Jacobovici, Simcha, and Charles Pellegrino. *The Jesus Family Tomb: The Evidence Behind the Discovery No One Wanted to Find*. San Francisco: Harper, 2008.

Jaffe, Dan. "The Virgin Birth of Jesus in the Talmudic Concept—A Philological and Historical Analysis." *Laval Theologique et Philosophique* 68, no. 3 (2012): 577–92.

Jasko, Andrew. "God Has a Narcissistic Personality Disorder." ExChristian.net. January 24, 2019. https://new.exchristian.net/2019/01/god-has-narcissistic-personality.html#.YNKjXehKi70.

Jewish Virtual Library. "Money Changers." Accessed April 5, 2021. https://www.jewishvirtuallibrary.org/money-changers.

Johnson, David Kyle, Ph.D. "The Santa Claus Lie Debate: Answering Objections." Psychology Today. 2013. Accessed 14 March 2021. psychologytoday.com/us/blog/plato-pop/201312/the-santa-claus-lie-debate-answering-objections.

Kaplan, J.T., et al. "Neural Correlates of Maintaining One's Political Beliefs in the Face of Counterevidence." Science Rep. 6, 39589; doi: 10.1038/srep39589. 2016. Creative Commons attribution: BY-4.0 International license. nature.com/articles/srep39589 Accessed 11 March 2021.

Kraut, Ogden. "Jesus Was Married." Accessed June 14, 2021. http://ogdenkraut.com/?page_id=133.

Kynaston, Gary. "The Mind is Everything. What You Think, You Become" Hammersmith Academy. 2014. Accessed 12 Feb. 2021. www.hammersmithacademy.org/news/mind-everything-think-become/.

Laden, Greg. "Why I would believe in God if I wasn't an atheist" GregLaden.com 15 Feb. 2016. Accessed 16 Feb. 2021. www.gregladen.com/blog/2016/02/15/why-i-would-believe-in-god-if-i-wasnt-an-atheist.

Lakhan, Shaheen E., MD, Ph.D., MEd, MS. "The God Brain – Is Religion Hardwired or Learned?" National Geographic TV Blogs. nationalgeographic.com. Accessed 16 Feb. 2021.

Lewis, C.S. *Mere Christianity*. New York: Macmillan, 1952.

Lutgen, Jerry. "The Talpiot Tombs: Background Guide." Friends of the Talpiot Tomb. Last modified April 10, 2012. http://talpiottomb.com/background_guide.html.

Maestripieri, Dario. "The Truth About Why Beautiful People Are More Successful." Psychology Today. March 8, 2012. https://www.psychologytoday.com/us/blog/games-primates-play/201203/the-truth-about-why-beautiful-people-are-more-successful.

McGrath, James F. "Am I Wrong About the Massacre of the Innocents?" Patheos. December 18, 2012. https://www.patheos.com/blogs/religionprof/2012/12/am-i-wrong-about-the-massacre-of-the-innocents.html.

Meggitt, Justin J. "The Madness of King Jesus: Why Was Jesus Put to Death, but His Followers Were Not?" *Journal for the Study of the New Testament* 29, no. 4 (2007): 379–413.

Merkes, Monika, Ph.D. "Bitterness Makes the Heart Grow Sicker" The Conversation. 02 September 2011. Accessed 26 June 2021. theconversation.com/bitterness-makes-the-heart-grow-sicker-2832.

Miller, Korin. "Can You Get Pregnant Without Having Sex? The Answer Might Surprise You." Health Magazine. July 28, 2020. https://www.health.com/condition/pregnancy/can-you-get-pregnant-without-having-sex.

Neuendorf, Michael. "Medical Artist Reveals What Jesus Christ Looked Like Using Forensic Science." Art Net. December 16, 2015. https://news.artnet.com/art-world/jesus-face-forensic-anthropology-art-392823.

New Testament Christians. "351 Old Testament Prophecies Fulfilled in Jesus Christ." January 20, 2015. https://www.newtestamentchristians.com/bible-study-resources/351-old-testament-prophecies-fulfilled-in-jesus-christ/.

Pianka, Eric R. "Virgin Birth in Human Females?" University of Texas, Austin. Accessed May 8, 2021. www.zo.utexas.edu/courses/THOC/VirginBirth.html.

Prather, James. "Taheb – the Samaritan Messiah." Think Hebrew. June 10, 2009. https://thinkhebrew.wordpress.com/2009/06/10/taheb-the-samaritan-messiah/.

Psychiatry Advisor. "Hallucinations, Optimism Help Maintain Grandiose Delusions in Schizophrenia." February 5, 2019. https://www.psychiatryadvisor.com/home/schizophrenia-advisor/hallucinations-optimism-help-maintain-grandiose-delusions-in-schizophrenia/#:~:text=The%20investigators%20suggest%20that%20optimism,of%20special%20ability%20or%20power.

Rayner, John D. *A Jewish Understanding of the World*. New York: Berghahn Books, 1998.

Rich, Tracy R. "Mashiach: The Messiah." Judaism 101. Accessed March 10, 2021. https://www.jewfaq.org/mashiach.htm.

Roth, Marshall. "Isaiah 53: The Suffering Servant." Aish HaTorah. Accessed June 9, 2021. www.aish.com/sp/ph/Isaiah_53_The_Suffering_Servant.html.

Sanglé-Binet, Charles. *La Folie de Jesus*. Paris: A. Malone, 1918.

Schechter, Solomon, and Julius H. Greenstone. "Marriage Laws." Jewish Encyclopedia. Accessed June 14, 2021. jewishencyclopedia.com/articles/10435-marriage-laws.

Shermer, Michael, Ph.D. "Patternicity: Finding Meaningful Patterns in Meaningless Noise." Scientific American. 01 December 2008. Accessed 14 March 2021. www.scientificamerican.com/article/patternicity-finding-meaningful-patterns/.

Shulman, Moshe. "Judaism and a Dying Messiah." Judaism's Answer. Accessed May 30, 2021. https://judaismsanswer.com/dyingmessiah.htm.

Staff, et al. "Cognitive Distortions" Therapist Aid. 2012. Accessed 2 Feb. 2021. therapistaid.com/therapy-worksheet-/cognitive-distortions.

Storr, Anthony. *Feet of Clay—Saints, Sinners and Madmen: A Study of Gurus*. New York: Free Press Paperbacks, 1996.

Strain, L., J.P. Warner, and T. Johnston. "A Human Parthenogenetic Chimaera." *Nature Genetics 11* (October 1, 1995): 164–69. https://doi.org/10.1038/ng1095-164.

Tabor, James D. "Who Is a Jew?" TaborBlog. December 1, 2019. https://jamestabor.com/who-is-a-jew/.

Taylor, Joan. "What Did Jesus Really Look Like?" BBC News. December 24, 2015. www.bbc.com/news/magazine-35120965.

Tennant, Agnieszka. "In Need of Deliverance." *Christianity Today* 45 (January 1, 2002): 46–48.

University of Southern California. "Hard-wired: The Brain's Circuitry for Political Belief." Science Daily. www.sciencedaily.com. 23 December 2016.

University of Oxford. "Humans 'Predisposed' to believe in gods and the afterlife." Science Daily. Accessed March 3, 2021. sciencedaily.com/releases/2011/07/110714103828.htm

Vance, Erik. "The Science Behind Miracles." Outside. January 16, 2017. https://www.outsideonline.com/2146421/limits-endurance.

Ward, Colleen A., and Michael H. Beaubrun. "The Psychodynamics of Demon Possession." *Journal for the Scientific Study of Religion* 19, no. 2 (1980): 201–7. jstor.org/stable/1386254.

WebMD. "The Placebo Effect: What Is It?" Accessed February 18, 2021. https://www.webmd.com/pain-management/what-is-the-placebo-effect

Wikimedia Commons. PDF: "The Jewish Encyclopedia, Vol. 7." 171. Accessed May 10, 2021. https://upload.wikimedia.org/wikipedia/commons/3/38/Jewish_Encyclopedia_Volume_7.pdf

Wikipedia. "Census of Quirinius." Accessed March 6, 2021. https://en.wikipedia.org/wiki/Census_of_Quirinius.

Wikipedia. "Church of the Holy Sepulchre." Accessed June 6, 2021. en.wikipedia.org/wiki/Church_of_the_Holy_Sepulchre.

Wikipedia. "Depiction of Jesus." Accessed May 23, 2021. https://en.wikipedia.org/wiki/Depiction_of_Jesus.

Wikipedia. "Edgar Cayce." Accessed February 22, 2021. https://en.wikipedia.org/wiki/Edgar_Cayce

Wikipedia. "Gospel of Judas." Accessed April 23, 2021. https://en.wikipedia.org/wiki/Gospel_of_Judas.

Wikipedia. "List of Jewish Messiah Claimants." Accessed February 19, 2021.
en.wikipedia.org/wiki/List_of_Jewish_messiah_claimants.

Wikipedia. "Massacre of the Innocents." Accessed March 8, 2021.
https://en.wikipedia.org/wiki/Massacre_of_the_Innocents.

Wikipedia. "Quirinius." Accessed March 6, 2021.
en.wikipedia.org/wiki/Quirinius.

Wilson, Tracy V. "How Zombies Work." How Stuff Works. Accessed June 4, 2021.
https://science.howstuffworks.com/science-vs-myth/strange-creatures/zombie.htm.

Winell, Marlene, Ph.D. "Religious Trauma Syndrome" Journey Free. No date. Accessed 04 Feb. 2021.
www.journeyfree.org/rts.

Yang, C.C. "Tetrodotoxin." *Critical Care Toxicology* (June 25, 2017): 2085–99.

www.ingramcontent.com/pod-product-compliance
Lightning Source LLC
Chambersburg PA
CBHW070907080526
44589CB00013B/1212